*Escaped from
the Nations*

Escaped from the Nations

Alexandra Glynn

WIPF & STOCK · Eugene, Oregon

ESCAPED FROM THE NATIONS

Copyright © 2016 Alexandra Glynn. All rights reserved. Except for brief quotations in critical publications or reviews, no part of this book may be reproduced in any manner without prior written permission from the publisher. Write: Permissions, Wipf and Stock Publishers, 199 W. 8th Ave., Suite 3, Eugene, OR 97401.

Wipf & Stock
An Imprint of Wipf and Stock Publishers
199 W. 8th Ave., Suite 3
Eugene, OR 97401

www.wipfandstock.com

PAPERBACK ISBN: 978-1-5326-0292-4
HARDCOVER ISBN: 978-1-5326-0294-8
EBOOK ISBN: 978-1-5326-0293-1

Manufactured in the U.S.A.   NOVEMBER 30, 2016

Contents

Acknowledgments | *vii*

The Visitation | 1
Shining in Our Hearts | 9
My Beautiful Home | 31
Crying after Him | 49
Pure Lovely | 71
Blessed Are the Meek | 89

Biblical References | *99*

Acknowledgments

THE AUTHOR WISHES TO thank Sofia Nikula, Mikaela Schutz, Peggy Glynn, and Aaron Wuollet.

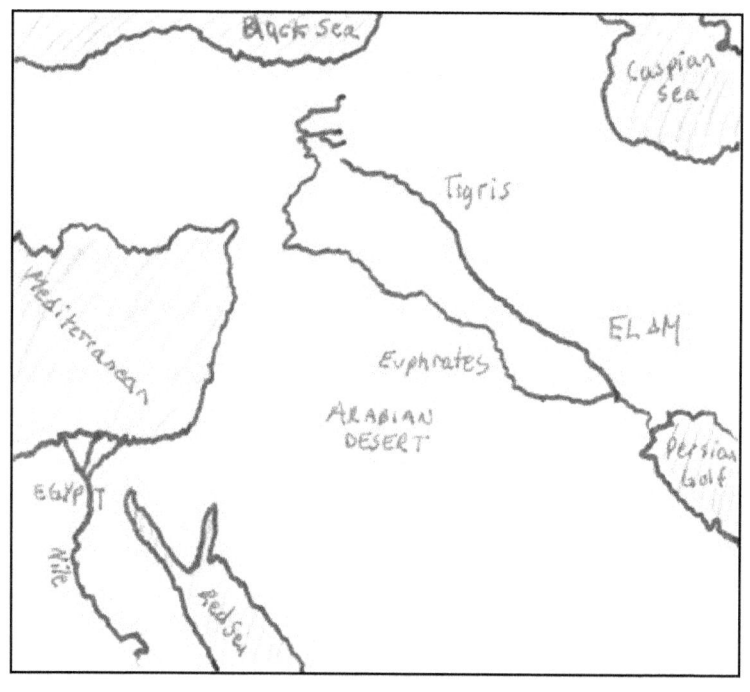

The Visitation
In the highlands of Elam, 5000 BC

1.

THE VISITATION HAD COME to our area in my great-great-grandfather's day. Now there were just a few of us left, gathered around the altar. God, who circumscribed the paths of the stars and commanded light to shine out from darkness in the beginning, had divided us from the others. We were apart, we who had once been one. Up on a hill, almost out of sight, but nearby, most of our tribe, many of them our relatives, gathered around another altar. It was an old altar. There the chiefs and spiritual leaders led those other people in a song that we could only catch the whisper of where we were, far down in a valley by a little lake.

Our altar was new, hastily built after we had been spit on and laughed at as we made our way out of the last gathering when we had split apart a few years ago. We had been set apart from those who were now on the high hill, by the beautiful shading oaks, with a view of the whole area where we always made our winter lodging.

Of course I didn't remember our departure very well. Mother said she wiped spittle off my little head, for she held my infant body in her arms, almost stumbling and dropping me, trembling, tearful, as she passed by the hissing on her way out of the gathering.

"Why did we leave, mama?" I asked her.

"Someone spoke the truth. There was an assembly of all the people in the entire area after the fall fruit-gathering. The one speaking the truth was bitterly accused. We said, we will listen more to the truth. They said, away with him. So we separated."

But, you see, we were only separated by invisible understandings. Because even though my best friend and cousin had gone with the other group, he still shepherded sheep with me every day. We fished together in the lakes brimming in the sun. We shot arrows together, we lay together with our backs in the clover facing the sky, guessing together how far it was to the moon, and speculating if any bird had ever flown there.

"No, it's too high," my cousin Sar would say.

"I guess I don't know," I would respond, with quiet discouragement.

But on the day of rest, Sar went his way, and I went mine. He went with his family up to the big gathering. There they were surrounded by large trees with leafy branches growing heavy with burden of fruit.

My group, our group, went down the sharp rutted path past a brine pit with our little handful. We greeted one another with a holy kiss. We sang, and one of my uncles or my grandfather or one of the others would talk about how the sacrifice on the altar was a picture of the sacrificing love our Creator had for us.

We would watch the choking terror of the little lamb while a turtledove warbled in the branches on high. Then the light would die from the lamb's eyes, as the blood from its heart drained into the cup after the priest cut its pulsing throat. The cup of blood was dashed onto the altar. Then we sang, accompanied by a flute, about the atonement for our sins by the mercies of our God. Sometimes the man who had come so long ago speaking the truth would come back and say the same things that my uncles or grandfather spoke.

It was morning on the day of rest. Murmuring waters fell down the slope hills around me and the altar. Everyone else had left the altar after the service. I sat by it, pondering Sar. When he came down the grassy bank by the creekside I was surprised.

"Why aren't you with your folks?" I asked him.

"We're done."

"We are too. What should we do?"

Sar shrugged.

"Ur, what happened? Why aren't you with us still?" He motioned to the new altar next to me. "Why did you all leave and build a new altar?"

"Because you had all been in the truth, but when someone came and warned you that you had fallen away you rejected him instead of repenting."

"Really." Sar looked back over the rutted and steep path he had come down to reach me. A fox crouched on the path watching him for a few seconds. Then it disappeared into the ferns. Sar motioned toward where smoke from the cooking fires went up nearby. "Why can't we go hunting with the bigger boys?"

"We're not old enough."

"We are too. What am I supposed to do? Skin animals all my life? Pretty soon I'll be helping my sisters sew."

"Oh, Sar, it can't be that bad. Mama says to give it some time."

2.

We worked all week. We ate well because I had a good fishing run. The air was cool and the smell of snow shivered in the air. I had no time to play with Sar. We only labored, side by side, tending our lambs, surrounded by everything that sinks or swims or creeps or flies, feeling the preparation activity of nature for the snows that were only weeks off. Some of the elders had gone on a trip to a neighboring village, so we had to do their work, as well as ours.

On the day of rest, mama and I overslept. We awoke at the bold note of a swallow that was like a stone thrown into a lake.

We were the last ones down by the creekside. As we got closer we didn't hear songs, but a clamoring of people. Nobody was sitting down waiting for the preaching to begin. They were all standing around what seemed to be a mixed-up pile of rocks. The earth was as if wounded there, and all around seemed to feel it.

"What is it, Ur?" Mama asked. "Go slip in and look."

I wound my way around bodies all gathered in a circle. When I could finally see what they saw, I saw the rocks of the altar, scattered and thrown around in the oddly multiplied light by the little lake.

I went back to Mama. "There's no altar. It's destroyed."

Mama lowered her gaze, moving away from the vision of the people, a betrayed figure under the hesitating sky. Behind her a few poppies in a small meadow laid down the law. She turned toward a huge tree off to one side of the meadow. As she stepped slowly toward it, I followed her. I felt like a spy in the very veins of the earth.

"Well, my babies' markers are still here. They left them alone." She stared down at the dead flowers we had put on the markers last week. Then she took my hand and tugged me down to sit next to the graves of my two little sisters. The forest stretched out behind her full of mists and mellow fruitfulness.

Mama's sister came up to her, fingering the wood and leather necklace she wore around her neck sadly. Her eyes revealed a mended soul. She sat down next to us. After a long time she said, "I wonder, who did it?"

3.

That night I didn't visit Sar. But the next morning we met at the sheepfold. Sar's fingers curled into the soft wool of the little lamb he held. I watched his eyes shifting restlessly, not meeting mine.

"Sar," I said, "they're going to let us go hunting with them next time they go, as soon as they get back."

Sar jumped up and grabbed my shoulder. "Ur. That's great news. Let's get to work then. They'll be so happy with our good work, they'll just have to let us go. They'll have to."

"It's already a promise. They will let us go."

Sar grinned. "But there's no harm in working hard to give them the extra reason to know how good we are."

I laughed with him and began leading the sheep to water.

We were going up the hill near where Sar and the other people gathered on the day of rest when we heard the drums. Sar quickly twisted around and took off at the sound, and was half-way down the hill when I caught up with him.

"Sar, Sar," I said, catching my breath. "The sheep, the sheep."

"They'll be fine," he said. "The elders are home. We're going hunting."

Sar pulled out of my grip and raced down toward the homes of our people. I turned back toward the sheep, picked up a rock, and threw it at a tree in frustration. There was the flock, on the hillside, gathered with a radiance all their own. "Stupid sheep," I said to them.

Two little lambs came up and rubbed themselves against me. "Silly fools." One of them seemed to be walking funny. I bent down and lifted it, checking its feet for sores. I found a wound. It was small, but it would get worse without care. I poured water on it and lifted the lamb up on my shoulders. Circling around the flock I watched for any nervousness among them—they could sense wild animals near. But they seemed calm, so I sat down on a big rock again, examining the little lamb's foot more closely.

There was still no sign of Sar when I finished. I closed my eyes. But the little lamb nuzzled my hand. "Silly lamb," I said. "Silly foolish lamb." I petted it.

As the evening came I began to sing. I had sung three or four verses when I realized there was someone else singing with me. It was Sar, joining in on the last verse of the song as if he didn't know how not to.

As his voice carried closer and closer, I could tell from his face that we were going hunting in the morning. I yelled so loud and gleefully that the little lamb almost fell off my shoulders.

Both of us were grinning enough to split our faces.

"Ur?" Sar said, suddenly sober.

"Yes."

"What did you all do on the day of rest yesterday?"

"Without an altar, you mean?"

Sar wouldn't meet my gaze, and he held his body tensely, as if to spring off like a wild goat. "Yes."

"It was just the same. We didn't do anything different."

"But how? You didn't have an altar."

"Sar, an altar and its sacrifice don't mean anything if you don't have the Spirit of God in your heart."

Sar didn't say anything. I might as well be trying to wound the wind.

"Do you know what I mean, Sar?"

"No. I don't." Sar flung his hand out toward the flock of sheep in their soft woolly clothing. "Ur, you're like one of these lambs. They bleat and bleat, and I hear them. But I don't know what they mean. That's what your speeches about God are like to me."

I took the lamb off my shoulders. "Sar. Do you see this little lamb? He came limping to me, bleating pitifully. So I took him up in my arms, and I have been carrying him all day. This is what God does for us. Now do you understand?"

Sar stared up at the coming of the starry night. The little lamb was warm in my arms, keeping off the worst of the fall chill. I waited for Sar, his face to me in the moonlight like Abel's must have been to Adam's.

"Sar?"

"No, Ur. I do not understand."

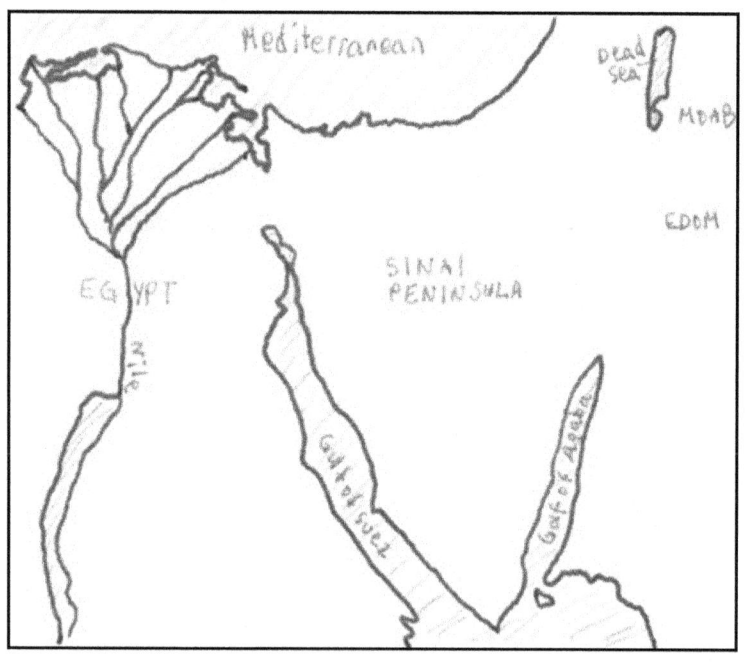

Shining in Our Hearts

The wilderness of Sinai, circa 1500–1300 BC

1.

THE FURTHER THEY GOT away from the palaces of Pharaoh and the hovels of Goshen, the more troubled the mixed multitude became. Around the fires at night, Beulah's mother had sung with the others freely at first. But, now, as the days went by, and they got further and further into the desert, increasingly Beulah's mother saw many hanging back from the fireside, drifting into the chill of the sepulchral dark of the desert night. Mocking laughter would sometimes spread out from them and find her as she listened between verses. "What about Egypt?" Beulah's father would mutter, as he tied up the livestock at night.

What about Egypt? What about the Egyptians? What were they doing tonight? Did they still mourn the loss of their dead oldest sons? Did their memories of the signs and wonders that had been done among them roam like lost beasts in their subconscious? Or had they gone back to the gaudy love of their priests, and their reproachless intoxications? Beulah didn't know.

Night had fallen like a blind cave. Lying in her small bed inside her family's tent, Beulah could hear the night singing outside the tent. She pictured the bowed heads and folded hands of the people gathered. She could not distinguish her mother's soft voice from the stronger voices of the others. But Beulah knew her mother sang, for the song they now sang was one of her favorites, one about lost children. The song always reminded Beulah of an Egyptian boy in Goshen. His name had been Thutmose. Some of the Egyptians had come to live in Goshen when Beulah was a baby, yearning for some peace and kindness. They had gotten peace and kindness, but also persecution. Many of them now traveled with Beulah and her family away from Egypt. But not Thutmose. He slept in the dust back near the Nile River. The scent of the trees and herbs in the fertile spot he had been buried would sometimes sneak like a symbol into Beulah's brain as she breathed in the still and dead wilderness air day after day. The boy had been kind to her, a few years older than her, but willing to show her how to help with the livestock, and how to play some of the games that the children used to play in the streets of Goshen. But he had died of the plague. Many young children had died of the plague that year. Father said he thought it was God's way of sparing them from the visitation of God's wonders and signs on Egypt that were to come. At least that's what Father said now. Beulah couldn't remember how he had explained the tragedy while it was happening in Egypt.

The front flap of the tent rustled. Beulah looked past the dead fire pit beside her bed to the little square of sky the open tent door revealed. Beneath it, Zillah's dark hair, tangled and full of wisps, shone in the moonlight as she leaned her head in. "Can I come in?"

"Sure," Beulah said. Zillah was a distant cousin and her best friend. She wore ribbons to hold her flowing hair back. It was snarly and sticky from her running around all day outside. Beulah's hair had no ribbon. It fanned around her face on the pillow. Her body lay spectre-thin and pale underneath some old worn animal skins.

"We are pulling up stakes at noon tomorrow," Zillah said, hurriedly and breathlessly as usual, her merry words tumbling out. "So I will have some time to visit you in the morning. But I came now, too, because that song is so sad and melancholy."

"Sad, but true. Why is the gathering going so late?"

"I don't know."

Zillah sat next to Beulah's bed and put her hand into Beulah's. Their hands were the same size, but one was strong and tanned from playing and helping all day traveling through the wilderness. The other was tremulous and weak from day after day lying in bed or being pulled behind a beast of burden.

Zillah's excitement was feverish, "The sky, Beulah, the colors—you have to come out with me in the morning and we'll count the shades of blue."

"I will feel too weak tomorrow. I know I will." The dissolution of her strength was daily more insidious.

Zillah patted her friend's frail and insubstantial arm. "Well, we can just sit here and talk, too." She lowered her voice, "What do you think of the manna?"

"The manna?"

"Yes, there are some who are talking about it."

"What would they be saying?" Beulah scanned her friend with kindred eyes and then looked over at the empty manna jar in the corner. They had eaten some in the morning and then had the rest for supper. Her mother gathered it in the morning, and put it in the jar. It tasted wholesome to Beulah, but sweet, too, like honey. She loved the manna. She had heard in a sermon once about the manna that God fed them with in the wilderness. It was manna to humble them, and to examine them and test them, and to do them good in the end.

"People are sick of it."

"How could anyone get sick of manna?" Beulah shook her head. She leaned back tiredly into the bed. The heat, almost like a kind of glamour, hung immanent around her. Her fingers picked at threads holding together the animal skins that covered her. Then they fell away weakly.

"Well, in Egypt we had a variety of food," Zillah said. Her voice sounded soft and blurry to Beulah.

Beulah thought about that. It was true, there had been cucumbers and lots of flesh in Egypt. She said, "But manna is good for you. It's enough. And it is a picture of God's Word of grace. Sweet and new every morning."

"It is?"

"Yes, don't you remember when we named it? When we first saw it we said, 'mah-na'—'what is it?' and so it got called 'manna.' You should go see if there are any crumbs left in that jar on the shelf over there. Mother sometimes saves the very last of the day's manna to give to us before bed."

Zillah got some manna, and the two girls ate, savoring its sweetness, listening to the psalm being sung outside the tent in the distant night where stars paved the firmament. It was a new song, a song by Miriam, which she had written after they had crossed the Red Sea.

When the song was over, the two girls began to sing, "The Lord is my strength and my song. He also has become my salvation." It carried beyond the tent, beyond the tents of the thousands of others, beyond the boundless horizon of sand, above, to the expanse, dark and unspotted.

2.

The voice of a man came to Beulah as she drifted out of sleep the next morning as the sun crept over the camp outside. The voice came from just on the other side of the skin of the tent next to her head.

The man's persuasive accent was soft, friendly and diffuse. He was saying, "Let's meet tonight. We're going to start journeying at noon today, and we will travel all day. We should stop at sundown, as usual. Let's meet then."

"Where?" another voice answered. This voice was deeper, and sounded precise and suspicious, but it held a fascinating elegance.

"How about right here? The people who travel in this tent are always gone. There's nobody there, they're too busy. And they have this extra animal skin hanging here to keep this spot shaded."

Beulah shifted stealthily in her bed on the other side of the tent skins. She noticed a little tear in the skin where the sewing of the skins had come loose. She reached out and pulled the tear back. Now she could see the two men talking. The man with the deeper voice was saying, "Yes, let's do that." He had wispy black hair and a full black beard with a little bit of gray in it. He looked older than her father.

Beulah looked at the other man, the one with the soft and friendly voice. He was much younger, and not very tall. He wore a braided belt, and his sandals were freshly made. His garb was that of the Levites, but showed gold filings in it that told of wealth. His face was handsome, as if a covering of beauty had been drawn on it. "Moses is proud." The younger man's voice was as if it dropped manna. "He has lifted himself up above the congregation."

The deeper voice of the adder-eyed man with the long black beard was muffled, but Beulah could still make out the words, "Yes, he shouldn't be in charge. Let's go back now, though; we wouldn't want to be missed."

"Right," said the man who wore the garb of the Levites. "Or to miss anything."

Then the older man, with the long black beard, stopped, and grabbed the sleeve of the kind-looking Levite. "Can I be part of the inner circle next time?"

The Levite's mouth twitched. The eyes of the hard-faced older man glittered. He clutched the Levite's arm convulsively, then let go. The Levite let his arm drop placidly to his side as each man turned away from the other.

Beulah felt drawn to the Levite's atmosphere of purity. She beheld absorbedly as the two men left the shade outside her tent. They each went a different way. The man with the black beard went over toward a large tent facing east. It was a big tent, Beulah could see; even from this distance she could tell. She knew that some very wealthy and important people tented there. They had many children, but the children were older. One of the youngest was friends with Beulah's older brother, Jubal. Beulah couldn't remember his name. But Jubal liked to go visit there because there was always plenty to do, and young people to visit. Much of the work of herding cattle was hired out with the people who tented over there, because the people were so wealthy.

The other man, the younger one, the Levite with the voice steeped in honeyed friendliness, was going toward the tabernacle.

It was a very large tent structure. In it the people gathered to hear the Word of God and to see the sacrifices, so that they could be reminded of God's sacrificing love for them. The man must be an important Levite, Beulah thought, watching his figure get smaller and smaller and then disappear into a gathering of people outside the door of the tabernacle.

What did they mean? Her entire soul felt blotted and gaunt as she picked up her sewing. Should she tell her mother? Moses had led them out of the promised land, she remembered. But he wasn't their leader. God was their leader. So what did they mean that Moses shouldn't be in charge? Moses wasn't in charge. God was.

Beulah lay there, her face blotchy, her mind confused, waiting for her mother to come back as the drowsy moments flaked away. Her mother and father always left to help with the herding, the manna-gathering, and the watering, early in the morning breezes. Her older brother, Jubal, always went with them to help, because he was fourteen. Beulah was twelve, and all her friends went to help. But she stayed in bed, sometimes hacking as if her whole lung would come up, and breathing with difficulty. Her other sibling, Enoch, who was only four, would always go over to the neighbor's tent to play with their littler children while the neighbor lady's mother watched them all.

The sun felt even hotter today, beating down on the crumbling nothingness of the wilderness around them. Beulah wiped sweat off her brow. It soaked the pillow under her head. Why were they waiting so long to get traveling for the day? Usually they left around sunup.

Beulah peeked out the hole in the tent again, waiting for the morning to elapse. There weren't many people walking around. Here and there a mother with little ones would hustle on by with a water pot, or a little girl would go by carrying something. There were tents everywhere, pitched close together. Where had all the people gone? She looked toward the direction that the younger man had disappeared into. There they all were! There at the front entrance to the tabernacle, the crowd had gotten bigger. More people were coming toward the gathering, too. Beulah couldn't see much, and she couldn't hear what was being said. But she watched for many minutes as the people gathered under the hot sun. Then, tired of holding herself up by the arm to see through the hole in the tent, she lay back, her heart filled with a shadowy fretfulness. The air in her family's tent was still, and flies buzzed around her. The little pot of manna that her parents had gathered for the day's meals stood on the rug.

I'll just close my eyes for a moment, Beulah thought. And she began to pray, "The Lord bless us and keep us . . ."

3.

"Crash!"

Beulah awoke with a start. Something had fallen outside the tent. "Is he okay? Is he okay?" It was her mother's voice, scared. Beulah's veins tingled.

"I'm fine, mama." That was her little brother Enoch.

"You gave me a great scare. I shouldn't let you ride on mules."

"Oh, mama, you're no fun," Enoch said. He scampered into the tent, and ran to Beulah. She weakly tried to hug his little lively body close to her.

Her mother came in.

"Hi, Beulah."

"Hi, Mother. Where are Father and Jubal?"

"Coming."

"Where were you all?"

"Over by the tabernacle door."

"For what?"

Beulah's mother came over with her silent watchingness and leaned over her pale daughter. Beulah knew that outside, around them, the camp activity hummed. Nearby little children played a game in the desert sand with sticks and rocks. The older children carried water and tended animals and little children. And everywhere the faces of the adults were weary but hopeful, like you are after a long and fruitful week of work on the evening before the

Sabbath. Beulah's mother smoothed Beulah's hair back. "How do you feel, honey?"

"Good enough, Mother. Why did you all gather?"

"There's no need for you to have anything more to worry about. You worry enough as it is." Beulah's mother got up and began to straighten the tent, preparing it for taking down and traveling. She could do the entire process in fifteen minutes.

Beulah sighed to herself. She thought about asking her mother again why they had all gathered so long instead of traveling, but instead she asked, "Is Moses proud?"

Beulah's mother whirled around and stared at her. "What?"

"Is Moses proud?"

"Where did you get that question from?"

Beulah was quiet, pallid, remembering the Levite's liquid-flowing syllables. "Does it matter? Is he?"

Beulah's mother walked back toward her. Her eyes were a troubled gray. "We are all proud, honey, every one of us. Nobody can say that one person is more proud than another."

"So why would someone say that about Moses?"

Beulah's mother would not answer. She seemed to be in some kind of transfiguration of annihilation, a durable soul-illness. She turned away, and went out the tent's front door to begin the process of pulling up stakes. For some reason Beulah thought of something she had learned long ago: stars are bright still, though the brightest may fall.

Beulah settled back in her bed in the blistering heat. She listened to her mother's sure movements outside the tent. Enoch had gone to the neighbor's tent. As she listened, she could hear others coming out of their tents and pulling up stakes. With her thin hand she reached over and picked up her sewing. She was making a little doll out of animal skins. She tried to thread the needle. Over and over she took the thread and tried to get it through the eye of the needle. Her hands shook. She rested them for a moment, then tried again. The end of the thread filmed before her eyes, blurring, and she dropped her hands down to her thin chest. She set the sewing down on the blanket in front of her and folded her hands across her stomach, staring up at the skins above her head as tears rolled down her cheeks into her dark brown curls.

4.

They were finally on the move again. Beulah's bed of animal skins was attached by ropes to a cow. The cow dragged Beulah behind her. Ahead of her, her cousin Zillah's rich blue and purple hem dragged in the dust. It was Zillah's job to be Beulah's companion, and to make sure the ropes didn't get tangled, and to make sure the cow walked at a steady pace. Zillah also watched out for rocks that might catch on the animal skin bed that held Beulah. Zillah was glad to help. Normally she would have been helping her mother with the smaller children in their family, but because she had other older sisters to help, the family could spare Zillah to be a helper friend to Beulah. Beulah's family had only her mother, father, Jubal, Beulah, and Enoch. There had been other children, six of them, but they had all died, either in a plague, or after birth, or from miscarriage. They were all buried in Egypt. "God will remember them even there on the day when he raises us all up unto himself," Mother had told Beulah. Beulah knew that was why Mother had named their last child Enoch. He was named after Enoch, a man who had lived very long ago, even before the time of Noah, and God had taken him up unto himself. Beulah's mother had expected God to take this little boy from her too, so she had named him Enoch.

"Did you finish sewing your doll?" Zillah asked Beulah, sweet as always, like a little brown kitty in a basket. Even her eyelashes were dusty, because the animals kicked up so much dust. With so many people and animals on the move, the whole desert around them had a little dust cloud swirling at all times. Far to the back of the procession, where they were, the carrion creatures lurked. Day by day Beulah's father tried to go faster and get up near the front, but somehow they always ended up almost at the end, with the slowest, the sick and the struggling.

"No," Beulah said, the dust sheening the mottled paleness of her cheeks. "I'm too weak to sew today. Where was everyone this morning?"

"Different places," Zillah said. "Some were at the tabernacle, others were gathered around drinking water where the jars of water are kept. Quite a few were at my parent's home, actually."

"Really?" Her tone was deferential, undemanding, but tinged with an undefined ache.

"Yes. My mother and father agree with Zed the Levite. He is a close work companion to Korah. They think something must be done to Moses."

"Who is Zed?"

"He wears a gold cord around his waist, you've probably seen him. He usually tents near our family's tent." Zillah went over to the corner of the tent-space where the food was. She lifted a gourd to her lips and tilted her head back. "This tastes so fresh," she said.

Beulah remembered the conversation between the two men that had woken her up this morning. "I think I know who he is. Short? Kind of young? He has a soft and friendly voice."

"Yes," Zillah said. "He has the gift of discerning spirits, and he has a list of all the people, including Moses, who he says are proud."

Beulah opened her mouth to protest, but then she heard her mother's voice above the din of the pack animals all around them. Around them the desert surrounded, ensnaring and unforgiving. She felt like Noah for a moment, letting a dove fly off, out of a window, wondering if it would come back.

"My dear Zillah!" Beulah's mother greeted Zillah. She had dropped back from her fast pace up ahead so she could check on Beulah.

"What?" Zillah asked her, warily, baffled.

"Zillah, I heard what you just said. That's not right," Beulah's mother said, her eyes unhappy pools, looking pitifully at Zillah. "Nobody should make lists of the bad and the good. Only God knows those things. He will reveal them in his time."

"But Zed does know," Zillah insisted. "He has the gift of discerning spirits."

"If he says he knows the conditions of the hearts of men, then he is putting himself in the place of God."

"But Moses really is proud." Zillah was angry now. "He is."

"Zillah, did your mom and dad say that?" Mother's voice was sad.

"Of course. And my mother and father are good people. They cannot be wrong!" The brown of her eyes shimmered with bitterness, stormy and scrambled.

Beulah's mother went close to Zillah and hugged her, as if by her embrace she could cause her to cast off her veil of distaste. "Oh, Zillah, I don't know what to say. It is not for our righteousness that we are able to go into our homeland with our Redeemer, for we are a stiff-necked people. But because he loves us, and is faithful to the promises he gives."

Beulah said, "We are all proud. At least that's what I have noticed."

"Yes," Mother said. "And Moses is doing what he is doing because God commanded it. Not because he decided to do it himself. Now I have to go up ahead and help again. You girls watch over each other."

"Okay."

When she had left, Beulah gently asked Zillah, "Zillah, do you remember Eldad and Medad, some time back? How they came and prophesied in the camp?"

"Yes."

"Well, they spoke about love, just as their names mean. 'Eldad' means 'God loves,' and 'Me-dad' means 'love.'"

"So?"

"So I am just saying, we have to remember love. To be charitable. To put the best interpretation on what other people are doing." Beulah thought about what she had learned of ancient stories. When Noah sinned after the flood, one of his sons went around and talked about it. The others went in and covered it, showing how God's mercy covers our sin and nakedness. That was love. She knew this, but how could she explain it to Zillah?

"Sure," Zillah said uncertainly, as if she yearned for her heart to twist.

The beats of Beulah's heart pulsed in a commotion of compassion. She put her hand on her friend's hand.

"What do you think of me?" Zillah asked.

"I think you're my wonderful sister that God gave me," Beulah said wistfully. She was still, as still as if somebody had switched something off inside her. Zillah's stumbling confusion filled her heart like a story told in hieroglyphics written all over a huge wall. Zillah was journeying along merrily with the crowd going to Canaan. But, will I get there, Beulah wondered?

Zillah twirled the ribbon in her hair and laughed lightly, "And you're my sister, too." Then with a final kiss goodbye, with tresses discomposed and glowing cheeks, she scurried off.

5.

That evening seemed sharp with waiting, and they paused for the night earlier than usual. Far away the bleating of a great herd of goats sounded restlessly. Beulah watched as her mother quickly put up the tent. Her mother's gaze was huddled, as if something ominous meddled with her thoughts. Other mothers were putting their tents up nearby. Soon Beulah's vision was obscured by the soft skin walls of the tent. "Do you want me to drag you outside so you can look around more? It's a while until bedtime." Beulah's mother's question was tender.

"Yes, if I could," Beulah responded, hoping the vision of the vast clear sky would stifle the sad unfoldings wrestling inside her.

As Beulah lay with her head propped up on pillows she watched some boys playing outside the neighbor's tent. "I'm going to put your eyes out!" a child cried.

"Like Moses wants to do!" another replied savagely.

Beulah looked over at her mother. Her mother's looks were covered with gray worry. She had heard the boys. They both turned to watch them playing. One boy took a rock and threw it at the other boy. It wasn't a very big rock, and it missed the boy by quite a bit. Beulah's mother started toward the boys and then backed up. Then she saw the child who had thrown the rock pick up another one. This rock was much bigger. Beulah's mother ran toward the child like a gentle minister of chastisement.

"Put that down."

The child had curly brown hair and he turned wildly toward Beulah's mother, surprised. "Why?" He sneered foully, like a bad inmate.

"We don't hurt other people."

The boy hesitated, then snarled a mean word at Beulah's mother. But he put the rock down.

"Your mother is tough." Beulah turned quickly. It was Zillah. She had come up while Beulah was watching her mother and the two boys. She had seen the whole altercation.

"Yes," Beulah said.

Zillah raised her eyebrows. "Well, I hope she listens to Korah, not Moses."

"Why?" Beulah asked.

Zillah was silent, because Beulah's mother was coming near them. She picked up a copper plate and studied her dim reflection in it.

"Mother," Beulah called, "Zillah wants you to listen to Korah, not Moses. Why?"

"Zillah," Beulah's mother pleaded. "I am not listening to the voice of man, but the voice of God. Moses is not my leader, God is. God led us through the great and terrifying wilderness, and is still leading us—in this wilderness where there are fiery serpents, and scorpions, and thirsty land, where there is no water. And it is God who brought forth water for us out of a rock of flint."

"God will decide these things," Beulah stated, her voice reaching out like an extended hand toward the turned back of Zillah.

"That's right," Beulah's mother said, a weary inscription on her brow.

Zillah picked up Beulah's doll. Seeing the unthreaded needle, she expertly threaded it and began sewing. "Oh, Beulah, I love this dress you are making for this doll."

6.

"Who's there?"

Beulah, who had been huddled under a sheepskin, turned toward the tent flap. Someone was standing there. In the distance she could hear the nighttime singing, like the murmur of yearning. Zillah had left to join it, and Beulah's mother and father and brothers were doing the night work.

It was quiet in the tent and Beulah could hear the labored breathing of whoever was standing there. It was too dark to see much more than a tall shape.

The breathing of the man outside slowed.

"Who's there?" Beulah repeated.

"Akhenaten." The sound came out as if someone waded in a river of sand.

"Who are you?" There were so many timid spots in her soul, but for some reason she forgot them all watching the solid silhouette move into the tent and toward her.

"An Egyptian. I saw your large group moving through the wilderness. I've been following you many days."

"We're the Hebrews. We are leaving Egypt."

"Leaving Egypt?" The man came and knelt beside Beulah's bed. Beulah's little jag of fear faded to nothing. She thought he looked like a good-hearted spy, and yet his eyes were lined with fatigue, as if his sleep was always filled with perturbations.

"And, child, why aren't you singing out there with the rest of them?"

"I'm dying."

The shaggy man smelled sweaty and dusty. Beulah inhaled in the deep night and leaned away from his haggard and woebegone figure. The man's sad smile revealed broken teeth beneath a scraggly beard. Beulah knew that banners flew high above the camp in many cases to indicate what was below them on the ground. The man must have seen the banners from afar off and went toward them to see what they signified.

"Who told you that you are dying? And how is it that you are dying, and I am not? Every tale condemns me as a renegade. But you, you are innocent."

"And yet the doctor affirms that I will die soon. And I just know. I am going from this life to eternity with God."

"Why are you on this journey?"

Beulah laughed starrily. It was like the unclenching of floodgates. She thought about the stately tombs of Egypt, the bustling marketplaces, the leeks and the tasty cucumbers, the garlic and the savory meat. They had all been drawn to the life of Egypt, its beauty and enjoyment. They had been slaves to it all. And yet as they slaved for the idols they had set up in their own hearts, it was as if they were being beaten by taskmaskers demanding good things of them, keeping a record of everything and hounding them with that record. "What should I say?" she mumbled in the darkness to Akhenaten.

A harmless snake wound its way over the foot of her bed and she shook it off weakly. Akhenaten got up and brushed the snake out of the tent and then sat down on the ground near Beulah.

"Say the truth," he said, looking like a raven in a nook, watching her.

"Well, in one way, I am going on this journey because my parents are."

"Yes, but did you want to leave Egypt?"

"Yes."

"And why else are you on this journey?"

"Well, in the sermons I hear, we learn about having a pure heart. God is leading us through the wilderness to know what is in our heart. To try us, and to chastise us, and to teach us, and to see if we will walk in his ways or not. He wants to know, is there faith? Is there trust? Not so that he knows, but so that we know."

The man was silent, stroking his dirty beard. The look in his eyes was decentralized, drifting, and Beulah could see this clearly because the moon was so bright tonight and the tent flap was open. The wandering fires in the sky moved with mystic dance and desert insects made their night noises as Beulah waited for the man to respond.

"God?" he said.

"Yes, God."

"Like Ra? Or Horus?"

"No, like God, the living God, the Creator of heaven and earth."

"What kind of God is this?"

"One that gives us a pure heart himself, and promises us good things."

"What good things?"

"Life with him. Life with him after dying."

"So you are on this journey to be with him?"

"As he has promised."

"He promised you? How do you know?"

"He speaks to us by his Spirit, in his Word. Why, a few Sabbaths ago, I heard the preaching of God, how he is love, and is merciful to sinners."

"You saw God? You heard him?"

"I didn't see him. I heard him speaking by his Spirit through Eldad and Medad."

"Eldad and Medad?"

"Yes, God also gives us many instructions and teachings, which are a blessing to follow. But we don't follow them. We find that we are disobedient, as God says in his Word, 'You have been rebellious against me since the day that I knew you.' But he is a God that pardons. He is full of compassion." Her voice was as full as the threshing floor at harvest time.

The man looked down at his worn and dirt-stained hands. It was quiet except for the desert birds gliding obscurely in the night vapor. "I am a sinner."

"You can believe your sins are pardoned by the living God."

"Is it possible? Can a man be righteous before God?"

"Yes. Man can be counted righteous before God when God looks on him with grace. Noah found grace in the eyes of God. You can too. Do you repent and feel sorry for your sins? Do you want to believe?"

"Yes."

"You can. You are blessed in the name of the living God. You can take hold of the promise given to Abraham, Isaac, and Jacob. It is the promise of the land that he gives."

"The promise of the land?" The man looked like he had a buried life and it was being dug up, one shovelful at a time.

"Yes. Long ago Abraham taught of it, and one just like you, Abimelech, believed, built an altar, and called on the living God. God's promise is the promise of life in God and with God, our Creator and Redeemer, forever."

Tears tracked down the desert man's dusty face.

Beulah took one of the man's dirty hands in her tender clean one. She began to sing with the song that was heard in the distance. The man was listening and rocking back and forth, saying, "Is it possible?" over and over. "I have been seeking rest even though I abide in the very throat of death. Is it possible?" Beulah watched and listened to him quietly. A bold dart of light filled his eyes—peace had sprung up in him like willows by the water courses.

"Beulah?"

It was Beulah's mother's voice. Beulah had not noticed that she had come in.

"Yes, Mother."

"Beulah, are you all right? Who is this?"

"Oh, mother, this is Akhenaten, an Egyptian. We have been talking. He is pardoned now, as we are."

Beulah's mother smiled uncertainly at the man, with all of her natural open hospitality.

"Is there peace to you?" she asked.

"Yes."

Beulah's mother ran and embraced the man. They both began to weep. Beulah thought they looked like creatures clinging together on a tipping raft.

"Do you have family?" Beulah's mother asked after a moment, letting go of the man and composing herself. The murmur of night-time shuffling outside the tent seeped into Beulah's consciousness. The people were returning from the night psalm-singing. She thought of the Levite's voice suddenly, subtle and unreleased.

"No." The man wiped tears away and took the last bit of the day's manna up in his hand.

"There is a tent nearby where unmarried men and widowers are living," Beulah's mother told him. "You could live there if you need a place to live."

Beulah knew the men that lived in that tent and thought there would be plenty of room for Akhenaten.

"Wonderful. So you will be near us."

"Yes," Beulah's mother said. "You will be near us in this wilderness, and you will see with us in this wilderness how the Lord our God carries us, as a man carries his son, all the way we go, until we come into our home. For the Lord our God has blessed us in all the work of our hands. He knows, close to his heart, all of us walking through this great wilderness."

7.

The next morning the people outside Beulah's tent started pulling up tent stakes when dawn had not yet started to color the sky. They gathered manna and filled their pockets, packed up their tents, and began moving through the desert, eating the sweet manna as they went. As night left and day came in, the pillar of fire that had led them by night faded away and the pillar of cloud came into view and led them.

Beulah lay on her bed of skins. This morning Akhenaten and her little brother were watching by her bedside. Her friend Zillah had left to go help with her mother's younger children.

"Akhenaten, what's that big mountain out in the distance?" Beulah's brother Enoch's voice was excited. He kept skipping ahead, then falling back, remembering his promise to keep an eye on Beulah.

"I don't know the name of it," Akhenaten responded. "Back where we were, closer to Egypt, I could have told you the names of all the mountains. I grew up on the edge of the wilderness there. But this is unfamiliar ground to me."

"We stopped at Mount Sinai a long time ago," said Enoch.

"It was a noteworthy event," said Beulah.

"How so?" asked the Egyptian.

"We received good commandments. Instructions that God gave us in love, to protect us, and to help us, and to protect our neighbor. But we do not follow them. So Moses took an animal, sacrificed it, and sprinkled the blood on the congregation, as a sign that through God's sacrificial work of love our sins are pardoned."

"There was smoke coming out of the mountain," Enoch's little voice broke in. "And you could not go near it. And if even one of our animals came close to it, that animal would die. I saw it," he added, with a four-year-old boy's importance.

"Sounds scary," said the Egyptian.

"It was."

"But what we are taught in the commandments is love. Cain did not love Abel. He broke the commandment to love your neighbor as yourself."

The Egyptian stared ahead into the dusty tracks of the travelers ahead of them like a seer of old.

"Well, I find that I don't love my neighbor."

"That's true," said Beulah. "But God forgives us our sins. He has forgiven me. He has forgiven you. After Moses came down from that scary mountain he sprinkled blood on the entire congregation because we all knew and felt that we did not do according to the words of the commandments, even though we all promised to follow God's words and teachings."

"There was fire and smoke and thunder!" Beulah's little brother said, picking up pebbles and throwing them into the dust ahead.

"Yes. It was scary," Beulah said. "But don't you remember the sprinkling of the blood?"

Enoch thought a minute. "I guess." He kept throwing pebbles. Then he stopped and went over to her, handing her a brightly shining black rock. "Here, you can have this one. It's pretty."

"Thanks Enoch," Beulah said. "Will you remember the sprinkling of the blood when I'm gone?" she asked him, gentle and delicate as a swan.

"Yes, I promise."

"You should promise too," Enoch said to Akhenaten.

"Okay," he said. "But what are these good commandments?"

"I'll teach them to you," Enoch said. "I know them. Moses teaches them to the little children and we write them in the dust in order to help us remember them. Here, stop a second, I'll show you."

8.

Late that night as the stars shown brighter than the jewels on Aaron's breastplate, Beulah reclined in her bed. Everyone else had fallen asleep except her father and Akhenaten. They had been talking quietly outside the tent for a very long time. Then Beulah's father turned to come in. Beulah heard him telling Akhenaten, "The earth, the world, it swallowed up Cain and he became indistinguishable from it."

Beulah's father stood inside the tent. He questioned her, "Do you know what I heard in the sermon this evening?"

"No, what?"

"That God loves the sojourning stranger, in giving him bread and clothing." Beulah studied his dear countenance in the darkness of the tent. He was like her grandfather, who had died in Egypt. She remembered how her grandfather used to tell her that a father going to visit his father always takes his children along with him.

Beulah smiled at the memory, and said to her father, "I'm soon going to be in the promised land. Maybe tonight."

Beulah's father began to shake and his eyes were leaden with despair. "Oh, my beloved," he sobbed, stretching his hands out to her.

"Father, I have not yet come into the abiding resting-place and inheritance that the Lord our God promises us. But soon." Beulah's face was dreamy and she reached out in the darkness toward her father as if she had no will to choose. "With all my brothers and sisters."

"And with God," her father said, his voice separating in the darkness, delirious with anguish.

"Yes, that was one of the sermons we heard before we heard the ten commandments at Mount Sinai," Beulah remembered. She was sure her father remembered it too. "You have seen what I did to the Egyptians, and how I carried you on eagles' wings, and brought you unto myself."

Her father looked at Beulah. He thought of his wife and the thousand decencies that daily flooded to him through his family. Now there would be a hole in his happiness. "Your pain and tears will soon be gone," he said feebly. Then, "Ah, bitterness. Bitterness!" Finally, the guard around his heart completely dissolved and he began to cry. He knew he would always hold her in the hollow of his soul.

Tears washed down Beulah's suffering face. "Oh, Father, what is going to happen to Mother? And Jubal and Enoch? And Zillah? Her hands are not weak. Her knees are not feeble."

Beulah's father could no longer speak. The wilderness wind howled around them. Thunder loosened like a stone, and then rolled down. The orange percussion of the campfires flickered across the landscape under the full moon. Beulah's father let go of Beulah's hand just as angels came and sealed the hushed casket of her soul. He leaned over and picked up the jar of manna. Then he turned back to Beulah. Her still face shone in the moonbeams. Her eyes looked beyond those faraway heraldic stars, he thought. He touched her cold cheek with a sudden gush of ungovernable joy. What did her new eyes see? What visions of the beloved was she beholding now?

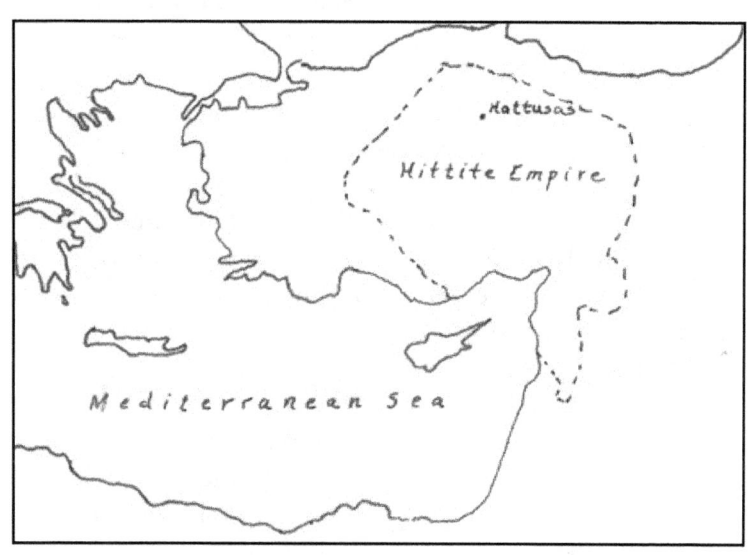

My Beautiful Home

On the road out of the Hittite Kingdom, circa 1000 BC

1.

"Tell me the mystery," Dubsar hollered over the pounding hooves of the horses.

Captain Gal's mixed smile was hidden under his beard, but Dubsar could hear it in his voice. "You believe there is a mystery?"

"If there isn't, then why did you say there was around the campfire last night?" Dubsar fingered the scar of an old laceration on his jaw and waited patiently for the answer of the tough warrior who rode next to him.

Captain Gal turned and scanned the little band of soldiers around them racing on horses through the tall grass beneath the purple mottled sky. He did not see his hunting dog. His strong voice rose in a whooping yell. "Here Zuzzu, here Zuzzu."

But Zuzzu was nowhere to be found. All Dubsar could see was dust and armor. Maybe Zuzzu was back with the packhorses. Someone might be throwing food away. Zuzzu was sure to find any soldier throwing food away.

"Captain Gal?" Dubsar tried again. "Captain Gal? Will you tell me more about the mystery when we stop for our evening meal?"

Captain Gal's face was the face of a mountain, his bearing solid, soldierly. "Yes, I will, young man," he said, "if you stop asking me questions right now. I have to get ahead of the company and look for shelters. Raiders and bandits are everywhere in this high country."

Worried thoughts kept straying through Dubsar's mind. "But it will be better when we get to the area near Kadesh, right?" They had left Hattusas, the big city of the Hittites, some weeks ago. The soldiers of Captain Gal trusted him; if he said they had to go around by the route that led near Kadesh, they trusted it was necessary.

"It might be better nearer Jerusalem," Captain Gal answered distractedly. Dubsar noticed the well-kept smile had fled the corners of his mouth. He was peering up ahead. His eyesight was so good, they said he could spot a beetle at fifty paces. "What's that?" He pointed out across the rolling hills to a little figure up ahead.

"It's a person," Dubsar noted. The distant form looked like a ship aground waiting for the return of the sea.

"Sure looks like a person. I wonder if he is friendly. He could be an outlaw." Dubsar watched as Captain Gal kicked his horse into top speed and raced toward the lone man up on the slope of the hill far ahead of them.

The other soldiers slowed down and kept their eyes on their captain. They stopped and let their horses chew the tall grass of the high plains for a moment, waiting for their captain to signal danger or all clear. A prudent crane drifted along solemnly overhead, as if swooping through wide arches. The rusting summer sky above was being eaten away, and somewhere in an untrodden region of Dubsar's heart, fear began to pulse. But the others with him seemed undisturbed.

Far ahead of them Captain Gal got off his horse. The strange man was wrapped in a mantle. His horse was nearby, crunching on grass. The man had to be a Hittite, like they were. Even from this distance, his horse and gear looked like the kind the Hittites had.

Captain Gal beckoned with his hand toward them that they should come toward him. He was still speaking to the lonely figure as the band of soldiers approached. Captain Gal turned to them and motioned them to get off their horses. "His name is Tushub," he told them, his tone haggard.

"Hello, friends," Tushub said. "I bring you good tidings from the land of Judah." He glanced at Dubsar and then returned his scrutiny back to Captain Gal. But in that second, that unfathomable short stare, Dubsar's heart was moved as the trees of the wood are moved by the wind. Inside him something motioned toward articulation but whatever it was failed to materialize.

"Judah?" Captain Gal was saying to Tushub. "That's where we are going. I hear they are hiring soldiers there."

"I'm a soldier myself," Tushub said. His eyes were gray, the color of cold ashes.

"I guessed that, from the way you carry yourself," Captain Gal replied. "One has to make a living somehow. Hunger and love are what moves the world. Is it true that they will hire Hittite soldiers in Judah? I have ten men here, and this one," he pointed to Dubsar. "My dead brother's son. He's only thirteen, but he can throw a spear with the best of them."

"And a slingshot," Dubsar reminded him, scuffing the grass with his foot, unable to look up. His whole being and soul felt established on the sand, constructed over a chasm.

"Right, Dubsar. Good son, why don't you take that slingshot and shoot us some game? We'll stop here for the evening. Have you anything to eat, Tushub?" He motioned toward a sheltered copse by a stream, the place his practiced eye had chosen to rest for the night. Tushub went toward it, the captain and the soldiers following.

"Yes," Dubsar could hear Tushub responding softly. Then the voices of the soldiers and the captain faded behind him as Dubsar turned his horse toward a stand of wood he saw toward the bottom of the hill. There would be game there.

2.

The doe lifted her head as Dubsar took aim. He held himself still under the willow. He had pushed his way past a muddy area through the weeds by a swamp that were like locked teeth. He had left footprints in the mud, but his movement through the tall grass behind him had marked no path.

Now there was a clearing before him. He heard the wind in the trees as it might have sounded at the dawn of creation. A field mouse scurried over his foot but he ignored it. The doe was alone now. The buck and another doe had wandered further down the meadow. The doe kept her head up for a long moment, then lowered it to feed. Dubsar slung the rock from its sling as hard as he could. The doe's head knocked backwards and Dubsar ran toward her with his knife drawn. Above, the clouds looked like they had fiends hidden in them. But it wasn't going to rain. Dubsar could smell it.

As he skinned the doe and cut the meat for hauling back to camp Dubsar thought about the man in the mantle, Tushub. For some reason, feeling Tushub's gaze, he had felt like a worm, the image of weakness. The old soldier hadn't been afraid of Captain Gal, even though this area was known for bandits. And Tushub's eyes hadn't looked like the fierce eyes of soldiers that Dubsar was used to. Yet his hands and his armor and his horse proved that he must be a soldier. Dubsar wondered what languages the man spoke. He obviously spoke the language used by the Hittites like a native, but it had a sort of accent of the coastal cities to the west, too. What about the language of the land of Judah? If the soldier in the mantle had worked there, in the service of the king as a warrior, he must have learned a little of their language. And what about his family? Was he all alone? He was an older man, but he looked tough. As tough as Dubsar's father had been? Dubsar put that thought away quickly, with pain implacable, into the subterranean emanations of his heart.

Dubsar cleaned his knife and then slung the meat from the doe over his back. Just then he heard a rustling behind him. He turned. Captain Gal's dog, Zuzzu, bounded through some saplings toward him. He jumped up and licked Dubsar's face.

"You crazy dog," Dubsar told him. "Come on, let's get back. There are deadly flies and hornets in that swamp over there." He thought about the stranger again as the leafy trees whispered above him. He felt as if he was scarred all over, though he was only thirteen and had had few wounds. In his heart, nothing was beginning. But something, something seemed to be beginning outside him, and seeping in. The gaze of Tushub remained with him like the weight of a claw on his arm.

The dog trotted ahead, and Dubsar moved as fast as he could to get back to the camp surrounded by the lengthening shadows. The hills were green and turning black from the deep pools of shade dropping around them. Dubsar knew that behind him the other doe and the buck had come back and were feeding just past the meadow where their fellow deer had just died.

"Dubsar!"

It was Captain Gal, singularly unamiable in appearance. "I see you found Zuzzu."

"She found me, rather, old rascal."

"And you didn't fail us for food, young man. Thank you."

Dubsar smiled mechanically.

Captain Gal took the doe from Dubsar to carry it into camp for him. As soon as they began walking toward the fire Captain Gal said, "That man, Tushub, is a crazy man."

Dubsar nodded doubtfully. "He seemed nice."

"Oh, he's nice all right, he's just daft. He thinks there is a resurrection from the dead."

"Well there is, everyone knows that. We always bury our people with items to carry with them into the afterlife."

"Yes, but he also thinks that there is only one god, not many, and that the God of Judah is the only God and that God is the judge at the day of resurrection. He says we should be prepared for that day by repenting of our sins now."

"What sins?"

"Well, there he is sitting over there, ask him."

As Captain Gal bore the doe's carcass away Dubsar turned toward the man, Tushub. He sat down on a log beside a little stand of trees watching the devouring and consuming fire. The dimpling stream ran laughing beyond the camp. The sky, faded and wan, was grim above, but holding back, like a proud steed reined.

"Hi, Tushub," Dubsar said. Dubsar had the kind of eyes that liked to look through you to the far distant hills. As he trained them on the old man in the mantle now, the man met his gaze soberly.

"Hello, young man," he said. "How is it being the only young person here?"

"Well, I have to do the hunting."

"You must be good at it."

Dubsar didn't say anything. Tushub contemplated the hazy smoke of the fire as he sat down on the log next to him. Out of the flames before him the sparks lingered and made sudden leaps. Tushub asked softly, "Did Captain Gal tell you I am crazy?"

"Yes, he did." Dubsar's face lifted honestly toward Tushub and asked him, "What sins should we repent of?"

Tushub leaned back, sipping from a skin of water he held. "Ah," he said. Then he set down the water. "Lying, stealing, cheating, adultery. Murder. Let none of you imagine evil in his heart against his neighbor."

Dubsar got up from the big log and turned away from Tushub. He watched the cook cutting up the doe nearby. The smoke from the fire rolled up in dusky wreaths. Dubsar turned to Tushub again as the man spoke, his voice full of a kind of seeking humility.

"But the greatest sin to repent of is not believing the promise of God, the promise that he gives in his Word."

"And what is that?" Dubsar sat back down, trying to surge out from the trance of Tushub's words. He felt infested, immersed.

"He promises to pardon sin. A broken and contrite heart he does not despise. He promises us everlasting life—he promises it to those who repent and take hold of the promises in his Word with all their heart. They will inherit the land." He gazed up at a hawk soaring overhead, and to Dubsar he seemed to be aching for wings.

"Does he pardon my sin?"

"Yes." His voice was quiet as a moonrise.

Tears began to come out of Dubsar's eyes so he wiped them away. But they kept coming, swift as jailed spirits escaping. He felt suddenly smitten, suddenly healed. He saw his sins as the Egyptians of Pharaoh's army dead on the shore of the sea.

"I was like you, too," Tushub said, still holding a stick over the fire on which he was roasting the flesh of the dead beast. "But now I am no longer a slave to sin, but I have a clean mind and serve the Living God. Do you believe the promises I am relating to you?"

"Yes."

Dubsar's face was shining from the remnant of his tears, rapt and enveloped. He looked around him for a company of angels, but there was only a battle-scarred man of flesh and blood. "I should go tell Captain Gal. Surely he will want to receive the promises of God too."

Dubsar got up and ran toward Captain Gal. Tushub followed. "Captain Gal, Captain Gal, I received the forgiveness of my sins and the hope of everlasting life."

Captain Gal turned with disconnected kindliness toward Dubsar. "That's nice," he said. Then he looked strangely at Tushub. "Now there are two crazies in camp, I suppose."

Dubsar couldn't stop smiling, and tears of joy began to come out of his eyes again. "Don't you want to receive what I received?"

Captain Gal gave a great exhalation. His quietness was vast.

"Don't you? You'll finally feel clean."

Captain Gal looked around. There were wild bears and fierce lions who might attack in this area. In this area, long ago, somewhere nearby, there had been a great battle between the Hittite Empire and the empire of Egypt. These plains had been thick with battalions and blood cries.

But now, over the landscape that had bristled with upright spears innumerable, the only sound was the wind in the grass and the hawk overhead.

"Captain Gal? Don't you?"

"Let's put this doe to cooking and eat, shall we? You can't eat wild grapes," he said.

3.

As they rode through the hills toward Jerusalem, many weeks later, Tushub brought his horse next to Dubsar's. "We're almost there," he shouted above the sound of the trotting horses and clanking metal.

"The city is right over that next hill, isn't it?" Dubsar pointed.

"Yes. Tonight we can gather around the Word of God for the first time in such a long time."

Dubsar smiled. He wanted to hug Tushub again. They had become closer than brothers, he thought. Over the days, the wisp of understanding that had possessed him in their first conversation had grown. But nobody else had wanted to hear the good news that Tushub had brought. Dubsar remembered waiting for days and days while traveling by the cedars of Lebanon for them to all realize what had happened to him and what beauty and promises they could receive freely. But the other soldiers went on in the ways of their own hearts as they had before. A few mocked him, but most just ignored him. Dubsar only saw that when they had wine in them, their speech betrayed something simmering in them. But he wondered at his own perception of them—did he really think they were always pretending when they had no wine in them?

Captain Gal was short with Dubsar, and clearly didn't like Tushub, or the change in Dubsar, but he left them to themselves as long as they did not talk about life after death in front of him, or the promises of God. Dubsar's thoughts often churned as if they contained a kingdom, and he felt like a besieged city. But discussing his difficulties with Tushub helped.

As they wound their way over the final hill, Dubsar saw the walls of Jerusalem come into view before him. They got closer, following a worn trail, joining merchantmen and priests and soldiers with spears to frighten the skies. All were entering and exiting the city, and many of the ones going in were moving quickly through the crowded streets toward the marketplace. Wool and jewelry figures, food of all flavors, slaves with their revolving eyes and awkwardness—it was all here. Dubsar had left his horse with the others' horses, and he had a few furs to trade. He walked through the marketplace, listening to the vendors and trying to keep an eye on where Captain Gal was. He saw a man leaning his head wearily against the side of a compassionate milk cow. Then he saw a merchant with a whole collection of little figurines. He went closer to look. They were gods. Dubsar pondered the little workmanships. Some were big and fertile-looking—they were for women to pray to, so that they would be fertile. Others looked more like warrior gods. They were a little different from the gods you found in homes in the land of the Hittites, but the concepts were the same, Dubsar could see that.

Dubsar was holding one of the little household gods in his hands when he looked up. Sun flashed on the metal over toward the edge of the marketplace. It was a chariot. The chariot-driver had harsh, Egyptian-looking features. He held a whip. Dubsar moved closer. The Egyptian picked up a lyre, sat down on the edge of the chariot, and began to play and sing a saga of heroes.

Dubsar had studied the chariot and the driver for only a moment when he saw Captain Gal and Tushub coming toward the chariot. They were walking with a man in clothing and headgear very different from the clothing and gear of the Hittites. He looked like a shrub with frizzled hair. Dubsar smiled and waved at his uncle. Captain Gal looked at him with relief and motioned for him to join them.

Captain Gal was talking with the man with frizzled hair. He was one of the leaders of the city, a Jebusite. Jerusalem was a Jebusite city, but there were more and more Hebrews there all the time.

"David is no longer king," the Jebusite was telling Captain Gal. "So you will have to get hired by the new king, who is David's son. His name is Absalom."

"Who holds the real power?" Captain Gal asked.

The Jebusite hedged, gauging Captain Gal's worth. Then he said, "Absalom. Those who follow him."

Tushub, who had been listening, broke in—"Wait a minute," he said to Captain Gal. "I don't believe this. I am friends with Ittai the Gittite, let me go ask him and confirm that what this Jebusite says is true."

The Jebusite shrugged, glancing around the mart of tribes around them with all its bustle and strenuousness. "Suit yourselves," he said, and wandered off toward a man charming a cobra.

Captain Gal's own unscrupulousness mocked him, but his masked face only stared sternly at Tushub. "What game are you playing?"

"None, sir. It's just that when I left this area a while ago, David was truly king. I simply don't believe that he could have been removed. Absalom was banished. And David's nephew, Joab, his sister's son, is the military leader around here. He is loyal to David. I can't imagine that David is not king."

"All right. I'll take Dubsar back to camp with me. Come back with news as soon as you can."

4.

That night in the hills around Jerusalem Dubsar laid awake listening to the murmur of the soldiers around the campfire. Above, the sky spread out powdered with stars. Tushub had still not returned, and Dubsar didn't like to be around the campfire without him. The language of the soldiers could be salty, and the stories they told could sometimes make people blush.

When the hooves of Tushub's horse could be heard approaching the campfire, Dubsar scooted his bed closer to listen.

"Halloo the camp!" Tushub's voice sounded loud in the night. A soldier raised a glimmering torch, but still Dubsar could see nothing. He imagined moles and bats everywhere. Were there any around? He could only hear the boot of animal skin rubbing the horse. Tushub dismounted and tied his horse.

"What did you find?" Captain Gal asked, handing Tushub a cup of hot warming liquid and taking a seat on a rock next to him.

Tushub's voice was, as always, like a whisper through the willow branches. But Dubsar was used to it. He listened. Tushub was telling the Captain: "I spoke with a servant of Ittai the Gittite. Some people still considered David to be king, some followed Absalom. But now Absalom is dead."

Captain Gal thought a moment. He very much wanted to leave this place with all his interpretations intact. He said, "So who shall we go talk to in order to get hired? Are they still fighting the Philistines? Are there many Hittites still in military service among the Hebrews?"

"Yes, yes," Tushub nodded.

"What happened?"

"Absalom rose up against his father." Tushub looked at Captain Gal cautiously. "They said David was too lenient."

"Too lenient? You mean too soft?"

"They say if he had been harsher and more demanding, more sly even, with his son Absalom, this would never have happened, this division."

Captain Gal rubbed his beard. "Well, they're right. He needs to learn war. The first one to strike wins—sly stratagems are the way to defeat the enemy, every warrior knows this."

Tushub's eyes were on the fire but he was not seeing it. "But love is not lenience," he said. Dubsar knew they were talking about different kinds of warfare, but he doubted that Captain Gal did.

Tushub went on, "Joab tells David, 'You love your enemies and hate your friends.' David doesn't hate his friends, but he does love his enemies."

"That's senseless. No wonder his son rose up against him. Who would follow that kind of leadership?"

Tushub sighed. "Captain Gal—" he started to say gently.

Captain Gal's shoulders hardened, he seemed to sense what was coming. He looked kissed by the dead.

"Captain Gal, it was also a matter of a difference of beliefs. That was the heart of it."

"Beliefs? Why should that matter? War is war."

"Because David believed one way, and the others believed another way. In fact, Absalom used to believe how David did, but he left that pathway. Now he is dead."

Captain Gal shook his head. "Really, this whole country is full of crazies, that's what you're telling me."

Tushub shrugged, throwing sticks onto the fire and watching them slowly catch fire and turn black. "I suppose that is how you would phrase it."

"I'm never going to understand until God reveals it to me, is that it?"

Tushub got up and backed away. "Captain Gal, really, I don't want to argue."

"No. It's all right. That's what you told me once. I suppose you still think it."

"It's not what I think that matters. What matters is what God testifies to be true."

"Right," Captain Gal's voice was tired.

Tushub's eyes pleaded with him. The night was silent around them, as if a destination was being revealed in it.

"Be quiet," Captain Gal said, his hand moving toward his spear. On the outskirts of the camp animals rustled. The horses were restless in the seething darkness. All of the soldiers in the camp reached for their weapons, remaining very still until the horses settled back down.

"Must have been a varmint," Tushub decided.

All the bluster seemed to come out of Captain Gal suddenly, like chaff blowing away on the eddies of the wind.

"All right. Pray for me," he said.

Tushub almost fell, he was so startled. It was like he had been eating dry bread for weeks and suddenly tasted sugar. It was the unveiling of a statue. "I will," he replied feebly. Dubsar could hardly hear him by then, and the shuffling sounds he made as he retreated toward his bed under the tree finally died out, as the night deepened as if it had been prophesied.

5.

The next morning Dubsar asked Tushub, "Do you think he meant it? That you should pray for him?"

"You mean Captain Gal?"

"Yes. I remember you told me a story of Pharaoh. When Moses and the children of Egypt were leaving Egypt, Pharaoh told Moses the same thing. He asked Moses to pray for him. But he didn't mean it."

Tushub let go of his horse, wheeled quickly, and hurried over to Dubsar. He gripped his shoulder. "Dubsar, the string does not always yield the sound that hand and heart intend. How are you sure Pharaoh didn't mean it?"

Dubsar looked down, pressed low with shame.

"How do you know what is meant?" Tushub asked him. Dubsar shook his head, his breathing suspended for a moment. His long hair covered his eyes. There had been no time to cut it, so he had it pulled back, but the leather strip he had used had fallen off. "You just love," Tushub said. "Now let's go. I found out where some of the children of God are gathering. We will work hard all day, and then Captain Gal will let us attend the gathering tonight."

Dubsar's archery exercises and tending to the horses flew by. But he had volunteered to do so much extra, that by the time Tushub came up to him telling him it was time to go, there was no time to go down to a stream and wash up a little.

When they got to the gathering around an altar Dubsar stuck close to Tushub, hiding his dirty hands in the folds of his garment. He looked over the crowd, trying to find other boys his age. There were many, he saw, but they all wore the dress of the Hebrews, and so he figured he would not be able to understand their speech. There were a few Jebusites and Moabites in the crowd too. Dubsar was not surprised. King David's great-grandmother had been a Moabite. Tushub had told him.

There were also people with almost slanted eyes. Tushub tried to decipher from their clothing and speech where they were from, but he could not. And he couldn't ask Tushub now because a song about malefactors was starting.

The few Hittites in the audience all seemed to be soldiers, he noticed, but they sang the sober but somehow ecstatic songs with as much gladness as anybody else there. It was like the singing and shouting of the grape-stompers at harvest time.

"What are they singing?" Dubsar asked Tushub in between verses. He had learned some songs on the journey from the land of the Hittites to Jerusalem, but the one he had just heard was unfamiliar.

"One written by King David, most likely. There are always new songs coming out, because he writes so many and they are so wonderful."

"But King David is a soldier."

"Yes, and a songwriter."

Dubsar thought about this, looking at the simply-dressed people around him. There didn't seem to be a lot of wealth, he thought. But maybe everybody just dressed simply at occasions like this. They all wore the joyful countenances of dancing children.

Tushub began to quietly whisper to Dubsar and to the few Hittites near them as the priest's speech began. Tushub was translating into the language commonly spoken by Hittites. Dubsar noticed that there were almost no words in common between the two languages. Tushub had taught him a little Hebrew, and told him that it was a language unrelated to the languages common in his country.

The man speaking the sermon was adjusting his speech to be slow and clear so that anyone translating would have time to hear and also translate. Dubsar felt the words of the sermon as the embrace of a home and a family.

The sermon was about the life to come. The priest spoke for a long time about sin and judgment for sin, but at the end his voice rose and he wept with longing, "Oh that I had wings like a dove! for then would I fly away, and be at rest."

When the sermon was over, Dubsar felt like a freshly plowed field planted with grain, waving golden in the sunshine.

"Tushub," he said, as he drowsed off that night. "Thank you for teaching me about the living God."

"It was not me that taught, but God in men. He has revealed himself also to you."

"Yes."

"And did you know that God has revealed to King David that the promised one, the hero who is to come and save us from death, will be born from the line of David?"

"What does that mean?" Everything, the trees standing sentinel, the shuffling horses nearby, the besprinkled and majestic sky overhead—it all felt spectacularly momentary.

"It means that our salvation will come through a descendant of King David."

"Really?" Dubsar was astonished. He knew about the promise made to Adam and Eve that one would come to destroy sin and death forever. But now it had been revealed of what race that promised one was to be born from? His genealogy? Dubsar pressed his reason into service, pondering. But it collapsed, and he was left merging and clutching in his mind. Above, the sun extended her last evening beams and the tired moon prepared to beam her weary way through the stars.

"Yes," Tushub said. "Remember what I told you about Abraham? That God promised him that the whole world would be blessed through his seed?"

"Yes." Dubsar stared at the constellation of Orion above him, then studied the entire sky, looking for a falling star.

"Well that was many generations ago. Now God has revealed that David, who is a descendent of Abraham, is also to be an ancestor of the victor over death."

"We really know that? That's astonishing, Tushub. It is an amazing time to live in. A time when revelations are at hand."

"But Dubsar—I am not long for this life. Hold tightly to what you have received, that no man take your crown." His words came like a fierce secret in the night, threaded through with pain.

"Tushub," Dubsar sat up in the dark night under the trees, his heart pounding as if he rode a runaway horse, "don't talk like that."

"No, Dubsar. I have sinned much in this life. I know I am now purchased into blessing but my temptations mock me and I wear a mask. I have brought you here where you can hear the Word of God. Sometimes we have to be like Joseph, and live far away from the teachings of God's Spirit. And that is difficult. If God leads you back to the land of the Hittites, I pray he will also do with you as he did with Joseph, and preserve you, and turn the hearts of your countrymen unto himself."

His words made Dubsar think of a baby sleeping, its soft hands curled up by its face. His speech had tied a kind of subduing power around Dubsar's fears, but still Dubsar could not fall asleep. He kept reaching out to feel for Tushub's warm wrist. The pulse was there, but weak. Dubsar's distorted soul had a vision of cherubim wings for a moment. Then he fell asleep beneath the moon whose face fills and empties each night. What was that song they sang tonight? "Thou tellest my wanderings: put thou my tears into thy bottle: are they not in thy book?"

6.

The sparrows' singing woke him up and there was the beloved face of Tushub, a statue of gray against the warm animal furs on which he lay. Captain Gal found Dubsar sobbing over Tushub's still body, folded like a worn old tent taken down.

"Dubsar," he said, "shush, now, shush my boy."

Dubsar could not stop shaking. A mass of mysterious griefs and joys coiled and uncoiled inside him.

"Captain Gal."

"Shush, my boy. It will be well."

Dubsar sobbed more, covering his face to hide his pity.

"You said yourself he is home now," Captain Gal whispered, his face utterly null, his mouth making an odd, delicate clicking sound.

"But now I am alone."

"I'm right here."

"Captain Gal." Dubsar's voice broke again, engulfed by a film of shuddering.

Reluctantly Captain Gal let go of Dubsar. "All right," he said. "I give up." His neck was an iron sinew and his brow was brass. He went and loosed a rope holding his horse to the tree. "I'll go get one of those crazies for you. I know where they are."

Dubsar wiped his tears again. "Thank you, Captain Gal." Cold drops stood on his trembling flesh, and behind his eyes a burning feeling shuttled back and forth. He knew Captain Gal hated ecstasy. He battled mightily for calm.

"Don't mention it. I can't understand it, lad. You're my own brother's boy, and you just met these people, yet you say they are your people, and I am not your people."

It was like the untying of a riddle, so mighty that Dubsar could not speak. He only nodded. He felt somehow that Captain Gal despised him and also despised himself for despising him.

Captain Gal's foot pushed into the side of his horse, and the horse took off running pell-mell through the hills toward the villages near Jerusalem.

Dubsar got up weeping and walked up the path from the camp toward the city of Jerusalem dazzling and tremendous under the warm sun. Over in the distance a day's journey or so from here was the tabernacle, in which there was the mercy seat and the blood-stained altar. Someday they were going to bring that altar and that tabernacle into this city.

The dust kicked up by the hooves of Captain Gal's horse settled on the dusty path before him. The city gleamed like a shell in the morning sun. Dubsar looked over toward the valley of Kidron, tears still streaming down his face. David had walked that very valley, weeping, as he fled the city from his son Absalom, as his treasonous son's triumph broke behind him, agonized and clear.

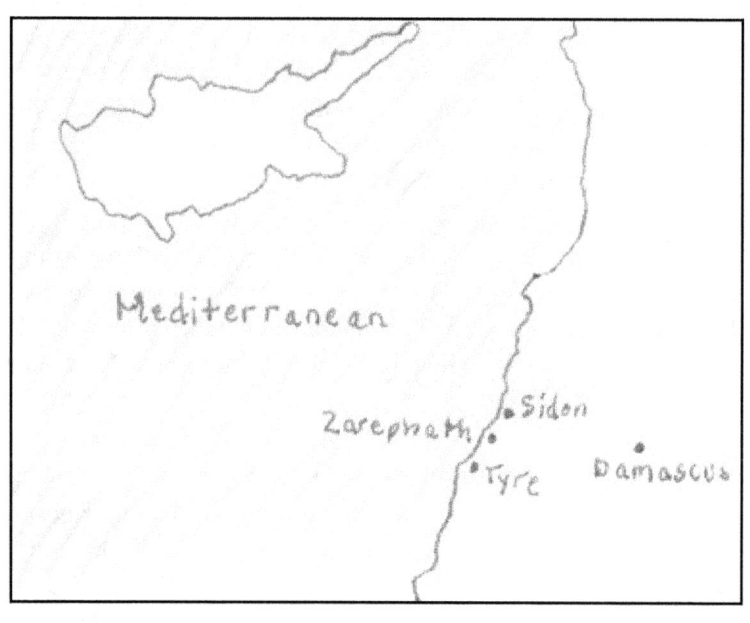

Crying after Him
Zarephath, a city in Phoenicia, 853 BC

1.

The morning sun warmly tapped the city of Zarephath. Hanno's mother was watering the flowers outside their home. It was spring. Hanno handed her his freshly filled waterskin and looked around toward the street leading to the central market of the town. It was dusty and empty except for a few old peddlers and some stray mutts. Next door an old woman gathered sticks from a little pile outside her caravan tent. Hanno watched his mother weed the little herb plot she kept near the flowers for a moment. The afternoon sun shimmered on her straight black hair and her perspiring face. Hanno sighed and looked back up the street toward the market. Still nothing. He ducked his head through the front door of his home again. All he saw was the bent figure of his older brother Ethbaal, his straight black hair as glorious as his mother's. But it was dull in the small room. The only sunlight came from a window by Ethbaal's writing table.

Ethbaal's scratching writing utensil on the document in front of him was the only sound in the room.

"Ethbaal?" Hanno said softly.

Ethbaal looked up dreamily from his writing, saw who was speaking to him, and then bowed his head back down. Never spurred, never fussed, he could shame the silliness out of anybody, and silence every gainsayer with his submissive earnestness. No maelstrom in him ever let loose, that Hanno could tell. Ethbaal's scraggly beard showed he was still quite a young man, only ten years older than Hanno, who was twelve. "But," Hanno often thought to himself, "he might as well be a hundred years older."

Hanno left his brother to accumulate enigmas, and wandered back outside and sat down in the dust, resting his head on his hands. He began to draw letters in the dust, practicing what he learned in the little hut school he gathered in sometimes. It was at the old teacher's down the road near the market. There was a wild rose bush right outside the entrance, and Hanno loved the place.

He had finished his alphabet and was starting to write a story when he saw a shadow come over his carefully drawn letters. Dusty feet stopped just short of the last letter.

"Hi, Hanno, what are you writing? The password primeval?"

"Pygmalion!" Hanno grinned at his friend's face, which, as always, wore a hero's winning smile. Pygmalion was like a cheerful and good goblin, right out of an adventure tale told around the fire at night. His amber eyes looked at life's valleys and hills gaily, curious what would come next.

Hanno glanced down at his story. "Nothing. Only a story about two boys going to the marketplace."

"How about three boys?" Pygmalion asked cheerfully. As always, he was allied on the side of gladness.

"Three?" Hanno fretted, gazing down at his story, then wiping it away with his dusty feet.

"Yes," Pygmalion replied. "I met another boy. His father is a merchant, like ours."

"When can we meet sailors? I'm sick of merchants."

Pygmalion laughed. "He's from Samaria."

"Samaria? There's no sea by Samaria."

"Right. That's why I know he's not much of a sailor."

"Okay. Let's go meet him. Let me tell Ethbaal."

The boys went through the door into Hanno's home. Hanno hurried toward the desk in the corner of the room and stood before

Ethbaal. Then he turned back and whispered to Pygmalion, "You tell him. He likes you better."

Pygmalion stood before the desk. Ethbaal was still hunched over his writing. Pygmalion stood by his elbow politely for a moment. He watched until he saw Ethbaal had finished a phrase. Then he said, disarmingly, his voice as soft as if there was a sleeping baby in the room, "Got to finish that copying job before night falls, eh? What is it?"

Ethbaal lifted up his head like a lazy tree branch in a soft wind and put his writing utensils down. "It's Hebrew, Pygmalion." His tone lured, pleasant and unthreatening. His pale hands were stained with dye.

"Hebrew? But it looks like our language."

"Yes, Phoenician and Hebrew are related. The alphabets are similar. See?" He drew a picture:

"But what is the writing you are copying?"

"It's books in Hebrew by Moses." He smoothed the flat space in front of him carefully, and pushed his hair behind his ears. His eyes were a withstanding metal color, and Hanno remembered his mother remarking that one could just about feel the crush of empires when Ethbaal got serious, which was almost always.

"Moses? We learned about him a lot over the last years we have been in school. So is this where all the stories about him come from?"

"Yes." Ethbaal studied the boys, somber and inscrutable. "Yes. I suppose you boys don't remember what life was like before?"

Hanno looked at Pygmalion and then back at Ethbaal. Pygmalion could always get Ethbaal to talk to them. Hanno wondered how he had ended up to be the brother of someone so different from himself. But Pygmalion made himself a kindred spirit of everyone immediately.

"I remember some of the old life," he said, uncertainly.

"You do?" Pygmalion set his hand on his shoulder. "Then tell us, Hanno."

"Before the Word of God came to our area, we used to be drunk a lot. I remember stepping in broken wine skins, the distilling intoxications. I remember wetting my feet with wine in the morning after a long night of music and powerful spirits."

"Right," said Pygmalion. "And the gossip was terrible, too, leading to longstanding quarrels, even murder."

"Yes. And very lewd behavior, a wide tract of sorrow," said Ethbaal. "It's good you're spared that." His eyes were gentle but Hanno still could not pierce a wink behind their surface. "I'm surprised you remember. It was five years ago."

"I remember when mother's heart was turned to be right, on the day she first believed in the promises of God. She went to many neighbors' houses and apologized to them for her hurtful speech and behavior. She took me with."

Ethbaal sighed, strung up to some impulse, and then released. He meaningfully flicked away a dead fly that had fallen down on his writing. Hanno remembered Baalzebub, a god, "the lord of the flies," whose wicked teachings they had followed.

Then Pygmalion said, "We're going to visit a Hebrew."

"A Hebrew?" Ethbaal lifted his head and scratched his beard. "I suppose you met him in the marketplace?"

"Yes."

"So last week you brought us to meet your new Egyptian friend. The week before that it was a Phrygian. So now we are going to meet a Hebrew?"

"Yes, from Samaria. But he doesn't serve the living God. He follows the traditions of men."

"How do you know, Pygmalion?"

"I asked him."

"What did he say?"

"I asked him if he follows the pathway that Elijah is on. He said he hates Elijah and so does everyone else in Samaria."

"Really?" Ethbaal sighed, turning back to his writing, cut off from them as if by a weaver. Hanno stared out the window. He adored Ethbaal, but he never quite believed in him. Outside, the dusty street was still almost empty. Everyone had scattered to their daily labors. Only when the sun began to set would the street fill up with those returning from their washing, their cleaning, their trading and their building.

Pygmalion ate a nut from the basket on the table in front of Ethbaal. "My new friend said Elijah is a troublemaker and a rabble-rouser. He stirs up the people and causes division. He stubbornly clings to his own opinions even though all the powerful people are against him."

Ethbaal's bowed head revealed brows suddenly wrinkled. But he didn't look up. He only said, "Yes. They are trying to shut him up because he is not following the important people but is sticking to what the Word of God says." He sighed. "So it always is. But it's not about two groups of people arguing. It's about light battling darkness."

Hanno picked up a basket his mother was weaving and worked on it. He thought about Elijah a minute. He had never met him and neither had Ethbaal. An old Syro-Phoenician woman who lived in their area had received a new heart because she had believed the Word of God when Elijah came and spoke to her and visit her. She had repented of all the sins that had been tormenting her for so long, and had them all washed away. Elijah had said that according to the promises God had given Noah and Abraham and Adam and Eve in the garden of Eden, God was going to send a chosen one of the seed of David, and he would wash the people clean of all sin and defilement. Many people in their area had believed because of what happened to that old woman that Elijah had visited. Hanno's parents had believed and everything had changed for them. But Elijah's message was widely hated and everywhere it was spoken against. Hanno remembered Ethbaal saying that if Elijah's enemies had been more silent, the fame of Elijah and the knowledge of his message would never have been spread so widely.

Pygmalion's parents had also believed. Hanno knew that beneath Pygmalion's constant light-hearted grin was a heart that solemnly wanted to keep trusting in the promises of God so that one day he could go abide with God for all eternity.

"So this is why you sit here hunched over this desk all day like an old man, hey, Ethbaal?" Pygmalion's question was insistent.

Ethbaal set down his writing utensil and leaned back on his stool. It was a movement that seemed to have slipped loose from him, and he contemplated the boys intently for a long moment. "To help people. So they can have copies of the writings of God."

"Do you know Hebrew well?" Pygmalion asked.

"Enough to help others."

"Tell us something in Hebrew."

"'Shalom.' It means peace."

"Great. So can we go to the marketplace now and meet my new friend and ask him if he has 'shalom'? Then you can get back to work?"

Ethbaal smiled, hazy and intangible. "Scoot along, boys. Come back before it gets too dark. And remember, not by force or guile. What the law wants, the will never wants, unless it pretends to want it out of fear or love."

Pygmalion and Hanno saluted him, looked at each other mystified, shrugged, and ran out of the home.

2.

As they approached the marketplace, Hanno put his hand on Pygmalion's shoulder, stopping him. "Pygmalion, stop a second. I want to watch the metalworkers."

Pygmalion was reluctant. "Oh, Hanno, I thought you wanted to be a sailor when you grow up. Not a metalworker. We should quickly go find my new friend before he leaves. These traveling merchants never wait around anywhere very long."

"Just a few minutes."

The fires were hot in the ovens of the metalworkers, far hotter than the ovens of those who sold fresh bread in the marketplace. The boys stared at the wild flames, their red arrows shifting and flickering around the workers. A man was pouring molten metal into a mold. He glanced up at the boys for a second, assured himself that they were safely far enough away from his work and then continued battering the metal into shape. Behind him the furnaces burned hot as other metalworkers toiled. Sparks flew, hurled headlong flaming into the dust to extinguish. One laborer set something down on a stool next to him, and a molten image hardened there next to a group of slaves. Dirt ran down their faces. Their arms were massive and polished with sweat. Hanno looked over at Pygmalion. His face was flushed from the heat and the excitement. The man he was watching came around to the other side of the table his work was on, blocking Hanno's view. Hanno turned away from the scene at the forge to look around the busy marketplace area. A boy about their age caught his eye. He was cajoling a stray dog to follow him, inviting him with a friendly voice and a bit of food. The boy came closer to where Hanno and Pygmalion stood. The dog, a small, pilfering, unprotected mongrel, followed the boy, whining wistfully for the food in the boy's hand. Then suddenly the dog gave a loud yap so that the startled boy dropped the bit of food. The dog grabbed it quickly in his jaws and slinked off. His piteous peal lingered in the street.

The boy's shoulders fell and he looked up and around the marketplace. Behind Hanno the hammering of the metal smiting the anvil got louder. The boy turned toward the sound and saw Hanno. Hanno nudged Pygmalion.

"Hey, Iggy?" he whispered. "Is that him?"

Pygmalion shifted toward the sheet, following Hanno's glance.

"Yes," he said, surprised. "His name is Benoni."

"Benoni!" Pygmalion called out.

The boy's confused look turned to pleasure when he saw who was calling him. He ran to them. Pygmalion hugged him.

"Here's my friend, Hanno." Pygmalion set his hand on Hanno's shoulder and nodded his head toward him.

Hanno tried to be generous in his study of the lad. Ethbaal often reminded him that fancy could produce a wild work. But the boy's expression seemed too weaved through with intricacies. He was aware of only a vague kindness emanating from the boy.

"Hi, Hanno. I'm Benoni."

Hanno nodded and blinked before the boy's clever and electric black eyes. The boy's clothes were clean but they weren't the clothes of the very rich. They were sturdy and about as tattered from rough work as Hanno's and Pygmalion's.

The boy motioned toward the burning forges behind them, his small hands fluid and sturdy. The loud laughter of the workpeople at their meals echoed through the streets past the skirmishing and scurrying of cabin boys. There were squalid-looking fat priests of Baal everywhere, and carpenters with wisps of wood in their hair. And everywhere, the beggars. Going right past them now was a beggar, a former soldier, clattering along on stumps. And here was another, a little girl with no hand.

"Do they ever give you a bit of metal? I mean, if you ask nicely?" The boy searched Hanno discerningly.

"Well," said Hanno, looking away, "I never thought to ask. But sometimes pieces of hardened metal that has flown off fall into the dust and they don't care if you pick those up. They're very small, though."

"But if you gather up enough little pieces, eventually you could get enough to melt and mold into your own design object." Benoni's hands waved all over as he talked. He was rather small and slight but he seemed bigger as he talked because he was so animated. "I would like to form my own coins. I would put pictures of battles on them. And victory symbols. Or I could make a ring for my mother."

"I suppose," Pygmalion mused. "You can't do much with just a drop of metal that has hardened."

"When I'm a pirate I'm going to have my metalworkers make me a huge embossed kettle. I'll keep it full of bubbling meat stew.

And everyone who comes by to visit will eat it with me, and no soul will dare dislike my reign," he added, winking.

"You'll be a very popular pirate," Pygmalion commented.

"But I thought pirates were cutthroats and cruel?"

Benoni's eyes were like murky pools in a shaded forest that flashed at Hanno. His shoulders lifted and his hands made a poetic gesture. "I suppose there are all kinds of pirates. One man's pirate is another man's merchant-ship captain."

Hanno thought of a gopher or a chickadee, running from here to there so sprightly and quick that he could not follow. "Where did you hear that? A pirate is bad. A merchant is good."

Benoni looked sideways at him. His energy was absorbing, and he brandished it far though he seemed not to be intending to. "Sometimes."

"What do you mean, sometimes?" Hanno made a face like he was towing something heavy. He wondered about the future of a boy whose chief motive seemed to be not to know.

"In the eyes of the people in the cities out west of here by Carthage some of your merchant-ship captains from Tyre and Sidon are considered to be pirates," Benoni was saying, his eyes like the merry frenzy of a dreamer.

"They're not! They're good. The merchants of Tyre and Sidon don't steal. They are not pirates. The pirates are pirates. Where do you come up with such ideas?" Hanno's words were livid. But his righteousness was dimming.

Benoni laughed, playfully anarchistic. "Listening to stories at night as the old folks gather around the fire."

He was clearly not totally serious, but Hanno was outraged, quivering and undone. "Well, you better think more carefully about what they tell you."

"What kinds of pirate stories do they tell?" Pygmalion broke in to ask in his usual prancing tone.

"Oh, lots. About shipwrecks and treasures, and kidnapped princesses, and piles and piles of gold." Benoni's hands dropped. "Don't your elders know lots of stories? And tell them to the children?"

Hanno and Pygmalion looked at each other. "Of course."

"Well, I suppose it does depend on what we mean by 'stories.'"

"What do you mean by that now?" Hanno's tone was grim as his helplessness grew more huge. "A story is a story."

Benoni's eyes swam in mirth. "Just like a pirate is a pirate?"

"Absolutely."

"Well aren't some stories true, and some stories not true?"

Hanno looked over at Pygmalion indecisively, spellbound, obstinate.

Then he turned back to Benoni. "What on earth do you mean? A pirate is a pirate. A story is a story."

"Of course. But some stories are true. Some are false. Just like some pirates are just captains of merchant-ships. And some are pirates."

"Help me, Pygmalion," Hanno pleaded, his tone plaintive. He felt like a misled ostrich. "And stop that sly grin. How can he say such things? It is unreasonable."

Pygmalion took a deep breath. He launched into a jolly explanation. "If you take a weaved cloth and unravel it, you can reweave it. The pattern can appear different, but it is the same weaved cloth." Then he stopped and shrugged. He turned to Benoni, "Tell us a story about a pirate and piles and piles of gold, Benoni. Where? Sheba? Tarshish?"

"No, no," Hanno objected, as if from a sense of injured merit. "First admit that the merchant-ship captains of Tyre and Sidon are not pirates."

"Would that be a story, then?" Benoni's voice was still so cheerful it made Hanno madder still.

After a clogged silence, Pygmalion nodded at Benoni and said, "A true story. Tell us a true story about a sinister pirate, fanged and glittering." Then he stepped between the two of them and patted Hanno's arm. He put one arm around Hanno's slumping shoulders and the other around Benoni. "Come, let's go watch the potter molding clay. Maybe she'll tell us stories. Then you won't have to worry, Hanno." He petted Hanno's hair. "Come, let's go." He turned to Benoni. "Tell a story."

Benoni's white teeth flashed in a splintered smile. "All right."

He began walking toward the direction he had come from. "Once there was a pirate off the shores of Libya," he began.

3.

"And they melted all the silver and weighed it in the balances, and it weighed so much it took six donkeys to carry all of it," Benoni was saying. "Well, here we are." The hoarse cadence of that old howler and scooper of storms, the sea, had faded far behind them and they faced the grouped tents of the caravans of the traveling merchantmen from many lands.

Hanno suddenly shook himself out of the story he had been in for the last few minutes, almost bumping into Benoni, who had stopped in the middle of the dusty street. In front of a merchant tent, a man sat, counting coins and marking marks in the dirt next to him.

"Hi, papa," Benoni said.

The man looked up. Hanno saw where Benoni got his deep black eyes. But this man was quite large of frame. Benoni looked like a pixie compared to him, even though the man was sitting. For a moment his face was clear, like a smooth stone, as if you could almost see through his brow into his thoughts. Then a veil came down.

"Good day," the man was saying. "Who are your new friends, my child?"

A little dog came up and licked Benoni's hand. He wiped it on his sleeve and then he motioned toward Pygmalion and Hanno, ready to introduce them. But Pygmalion spoke up first. "I'm Pygmalion," he said. "This is Hanno. We're from here, most of the time. We were born here. We are Phoenicians."

"Well, we are just visiting Zarephath." The man's voice was deep and clear, avid.

"Yes," Pygmalion said. "You are from Samaria. We have heard of it. That is where Elijah is from. We believe like he does." The little dog went over from Benoni and licked Benoni's father's hand too.

Benoni's father's expression changed, tomb-like, preyed-upon. His eyes turned toward the boys, burning balefully. He looked at his son. Each read in the other's countenance his own dismay. "Where is Elijah hiding? That man should be punished."

Hanno was shocked at the man's wrath, like the darkness visible of a forge. "He's only teaching us the way of life, the way that Adam and Abel and Seth followed." Hanno's voice became shy. "It is simply the faith of Enoch, that we shall one day be gathered up to be with God when our life ends if we hold on to his promises until death."

"Where is Elijah?"

"How should we know? We've never met him."

Pygmalion took the little dog up into his arms and said, "How is it that you, being Hebrews, do not know these things?"

"What things?" Benoni asked, sitting down next to his father to trace in the dust.

Hanno explained patiently. "The seed of the woman which will come and crush the head of the serpent will be of the tribe of David, of Judah, of the Hebrews. So he will be one of you. How is it that you do not know this?"

"We have the blood of Abraham in our veins," Benoni's father's response was like the slash of a sword, yet he kept on stroking his beard, so contained and controlled that Hanno became nervous. "We are Hebrews." Benoni sat moored to the ground. He stopped tracing, gnawed at by some kind of absence.

"Well, the heart of man is evil from his youth, the teaching of God says, so what are you going to do to defend yourself from your own sins when you die? What will you do at the judgment, you who do his errands in this world now?"

"I can't believe this Elijah-doctrine is being taught even this far away from Israel," Benoni's father said. He wanted many things, and loathed it.

Hanno fervently wished Ethbaal were there. But he said, "Well, when letters were sent to warn all those other kingdoms about Elijah, all they did was stir up curiosity. So even the hatred of God was used to further God's work."

"Is that how you got messed up in the teachings of that proud man?"

"What?"

"He asserts and asserts, and says we are wrong and he is right. Like he knows everything."

"Well, it is not him. It is the Spirit of God in him. They are not opposing you, but me, Moses said."

"Get out." Benoni's father's eyes were weapons with menacing points and yet somehow piteous as he stood up, messing up his careful calculations in the dust. There was something handled and used about him, Hanno thought. He was wearied and bled, thin with consciousness.

"Get out of here. Leave." It was like a putrefying sore. Pygmalion took Hanno's hand and led him away.

As they walked down the road they heard the father telling his son. "You must never speak with those people again."

As the occasion slipped away, with the voices fading behind them, Hanno's fright went out of him like a crushed candle.

4.

"I think I know why he hates Elijah so much," Hanno said as the boys trudged toward the harbor. Ahead a wary soldier stood staring toward the ships, as if pondering his voyage. A group of galley slaves, chained together, trooped by, as behind them in the harbor waited the ships, drifting with sails furled. An old woman, her face smoothed by hypocrisy, knitted in a doorway nearby and marked each one who passed.

"A conscience burrowing like a mole away from itself," Pygmalion responded.

"Yes, and he hates that Elijah says there is only one way of faith and that man is not in it."

"True," Pygmalion reflected.

"Yes," said Hanno, with oceanic feeling. "But maybe there is hope for the little boy, for Benoni."

"Hanno," Pygmalion stopped. Ahead of them were the sails dotting the harbor. The ships brought trade from the far frontiers of the great Phoenician sea empire. Here they were, near its heart. The clamor of overseers hollering and whipping the heavy-burdened souls who loaded and unloaded the ships surrounded them. Hanno glanced over at Pygmalion and Pygmalion wasn't looking at the ships with their bright banners. He was looking at Hanno as one who cleared the dark senses of others.

"What?"

"Can't you love anybody?"

"Of course."

"Why do you have hope for the son, but not the father?"

"Well, I guess I don't know. He just seemed more open."

"Can you look into his heart?"

"No. Of course not."

"Do you always know what people mean when they say things? Do you always know why they say what they say?"

"No."

"Hanno," Pygmalion pointed to a man who had just staggered out of a drinking-shop and collapsed in the dust in front of it. A dog came and sniffed at him, then wandered off. Workers and sailors stepped over him, rudely kicking the man's body. His face was turned toward the earth in front of Hanno and Pygmalion with a kind of leering drudgery.

"Hanno, do you see that man in the dust there?" His merry-hearted voice was more serious than Hanno had ever heard it.

"Yes."

"There's hope for him. There's hope for him and there's hope for Benoni and for Benoni's father."

Hanno sighed, looking like an abandoned field gone to ruin. The remembrance of the hostility of Benoni's father had not faded.

Pygmalion, overflowing with affectionateness, put his arm around Hanno's shoulder and steered him toward the drunk.

Pygmalion leaned over the tattered figure and tapped him on the shoulder.

The man's brutish eyes blinked as if it could never be dark enough for him, "Eh?"

"Hi. I'm Pygmalion. This is Hanno. Good to meet you. Do you need some help, sir?"

The man scowled. Hanno could see that his friend had caught him with that intimacy of mind and soul that Pygmalion possessed. But the broken man swayed away from him, "Get lost, brats." He stumbled to his feet. Then he turned again to look at them through his sunken, watery eyes.

Pygmalion held his gaze and smiled his smile that could muffle the murmuring of every restless soul. The man turned away from the boy again, confused, and hobbled back toward the drinking-hut.

The stray dog followed the man in and Pygmalion put his arm back around Hanno's shoulders. "Let's go look at the ships."

When the boys got to the water's edge they found an out-of-the-way place and sat to watch the bustling activity of the dockyards. There were huge slaves, and little scribbling clerks counting the loads. Most of the languages were unintelligible to the boys.

But some of it they understood.

"Wow, some pretty bad language around here," Hanno noted.

Pygmalion was quiet. He was watching as a curly-haired Greek man talked to a boy who was about their age. The boy was leaning on a cane.

"Is that a beggar?" Pygmalion asked Hanno, motioning toward the two figures.

"No. I think the older guy is that boy's dad."

"Why is the boy walking funny?"

"Is he?"

"Yes, look at the stick he leans on every time he takes a step."

The boys watched as the older man shielded his eyes and looked out over the water as the lame boy pointed to the ships, winged and waiting in the salty liquid that rocked them.

Then the blighted boy and the man turned and began to make their way slowly in the direction of Pygmalion and Hanno. The bony-limbed boy limped and used his cane both to help him walk and also to motion excitedly with. Then the two figures went past Hanno and Pygmalion and began to disappear into the crowds on the pier.

"Did you see that boy's face?" Hanno inquired.

"Yes."

"There's something wrong with him."

"Maybe he was captured and tortured by pirates."

"No," Hanno said. "I've seen that look before. He's blessed."

"Blessed? A courier cherub?"

"He isn't right in the head. He's like a child."

"Yes," said Pygmalion. He had picked up a handful of dust off the road and was casting it behind his back as they went. "That makes sense. I guess I have seen people with that look before. What a hard life."

"No, not really."

"Well, yes, I suppose." Pygmalion wiped his hands on the old piece of cloth he wore. "People can be cruel to you and that's hard. But you always have a clean conscience."

Hanno knew it would be nice to be always simple-minded. He often wished he had something to blindfold his unhappiness when he saw how wicked the world was.

"I wonder what he would say about Benoni."

"I doubt we could understand him. Could you tell what those two were saying?

"No."

"What do you think Benoni would say of him?"

Pygmalion laughed. "Something having to do with pirates, most likely."

"Do you think we'll ever be bold enough to talk to one?"

"A pirate?"

"Yes."

Pygmalion looked around at the crowded mess of action around them on the harbor. He scanned the ships cradled on the water, the heavens spread out above them like a huge tent. "I kind of agree with Benoni. Some of these people around us are probably pirates but we don't know. We think they are good if they come from the land of our people."

Just then a particularly fearsome man bumped into him. He had big gold wrist-bracelets and was followed by two hulking slaves. He smelled like spices from Arabia.

"Excuse me, sir," Pygmalion stopped him.

Hanno grabbed his friend and tried to drag him away, shushing him. But Pygmalion held his ground, immune, an aristocrat of glee.

Pygmalion faced the man, who had stopped and was smirking at them, lucid and lurid. "Sir, are you a pirate?"

The man's smile broke, revealing shining teeth. He must be young, Hanno thought. His ebony eyes were something rich and strange. "Of course I'm a pirate." His voice was rough. "In the service of the priests and kings of Sidon." He laughed and Pygmalion furrowed his brow uncertainly.

"Excuse me. Thank you, sir."

"On your way now with you, boys. You're too young to be pirates." The man swaggered off and the two slaves followed, their skin brown and dusty in the waning evening light, as the ships sloped their pointing spires on the water beyond.

5.

The wan moon rose over the white waves behind them as the boys walked home. Hanno thought about the pirate. He hadn't had a sword, but he had looked like he would chain anyone to a burning lake. And yet, didn't all pirates have swords, or daggers at least? But maybe he had left it on his ship with his other dark designs. Hanno's father had once gone to Damascus and had come back with stories of a merchant who sold only daggers.

"Did you see the Cretans?" Pygmalion asked.

"Yes, why?"

"No reason. It's just that I hope to go to Crete some day. That's where the story of the labyrinth is from."

Pygmalion was rubbing his eyes as they went into Hanno's house.

Hanno's mother sat sewing by the light of a little oil lamp, and Ethbaal was sitting across from her so he could see for just a few more minutes in the dusky air.

"How was your day, boys?" Hanno's mother inquired.

Hanno shrugged and fixed his eyes on a corner of the dirt floor. "Okay, I guess."

Pygmalion went near Ethbaal's writing desk, as from outside the soft melody of a passing flute player floated in.

Pygmalion watched for a while. "Ethbaal," he said softly then, touching his shoulder as friendly as the little puppy they had seen with Benoni.

Ethbaal gave in, glancing one last time at the text before him. Then turning to Pygmalion, an unsolved parable in his eyes, he asked him, "What is it, friend?"

"Do you know any stories about pirates?"

"Pirates. You want a story about pirates. Havoc and spoil and ruin are the game of pirates. You still want one about them?"

Just then, hollow footsteps were heard outside. There was a knocking sound. The boys looked fearful. People rarely knocked on doors around here this late. Hanno went toward the door, about to open it. Then he looked back at his mother.

A great surge of comprehension began to beat at Hanno's face, and then his mother whispered, "Let him in, lest we drive an angel from our door."

Hanno opened the door mutely. Benoni stood there in the dim shadows. He merged into the room past Hanno and stood gazing at them for a moment, securing a kind of dominion. Hanno felt scrutinized, summed up. Then Benoni spoke, his voice almost delirious with pleading, "Oh, think not my father a base foul stone set in a gold ring! For he was a debt-slave from birth. And it came to pass not long ago that he was able to pay the debt off. But he cannot forget the abuse of his master, a bitter and clawing man."

"It is okay," Hanno's mother said. "We understand. In a way, we were debt-slaves ourselves not long ago. Won't you have some water, or a meal?"

"No," Benoni said, his wise eyes flaring a signal. "I only came to apologize and explain. Last night my father dreamed he was at a banquet but he awoke hungry." His eyes searched them, as if seeking an interpretation of the dream from them. Then he turned abruptly to the door and put his hand on the latch. "Now I must go." He tipped his head as if listening to a silent prayer. Then he went out into the abyss of night.

There was a tense, abstract pause. Pygmalion and Hanno turned to Ethbaal, clutchingly. An upheaval flickered in the scholar's soul for a second, and was gone. His gaze was a sealed scroll. Failing to find some suitable phrase to address the revelations of the boy, he sighed, and said to them, "A story? How about one about a sailor?"

"No. Sailors are boring." Somehow Hanno felt as if everyone in the room was being counted, and he wanted to slink away, maybe to see where Benoni had gone. He felt as if a hidden lock had come into view but he couldn't discern it fully. It was like a letter, a message that he had held onto for a long time, not knowing who it was for. He suddenly saw the name, boldly spelled.

"Okay, a priest then," Pygmalion said.

"Yes," Hanno said from across the room. His brow felt tight. "Tell us a story about a priest."

"A priest of Baal," said Pygmalion.

"Well, then," said Ethbaal with the expression of a troubadour whose song nobody ever listens to. "It will be a very scary story." He put down his writing utensil with sage deliberateness. "Once there was a priest of Baal. He always wore white. Whenever he slaughtered animals for sacrifices the blood would get on his clean white linen. So one day he decided to capture two boys and make them live in a cage and clean his robes all day every day. So from that day on he watched for boys who came into his temple. Finally he caught two. He chained them and put them to work cleaning. And I believe those boys are still chained up working for that priest to this day. And so now his clothes are always white. So everyone who sees him sees only the clear white. But nobody knows about the boys in the cage in the temple of Baal."

"Well, then how do you know about the boys?" Pygmalion asked Ethbaal with a gamboling smile.

Ethbaal only raised his eyebrows in great bareness of manner, tipped his head back down, and went back to writing. A nightingale began her night remembrancing song outside where the threads that connect the stars remained invisible.

Pygmalion was not to be thwarted so easily. He pressed Ethbaal again. "How can the priests of Baal do sacrifice and so do the Hebrews in the temple at Jerusalem? What's the difference?"

Ethbaal stopped, and started putting away his work for the night. He blew out the little flame on the table. The sounds of the street outside were dim, the harbor and the marketplace seemed far off, the fast and exciting glory of the harbor withered away. Charity's battle for mastery overwhelmed the souls in the room. There were no heaving shadows, only substance, a wealth of comprehension and discernment.

Ethbaal began, "Because of the condition of heart of those who hear the Word at the sacrifices. That's the difference. A sacrifice is a picture of God's sacrificing love to redeem man from sin. Whoever believes this as the Word of God teaches, he is at the sacrifice in the right way, and he sees in the sacrifice that which is meant to be seen. It is what God meant when he set up sacrifice for Adam and Eve."

"Yes, the seed of the woman who will come and crush the head of the serpent."

"Yes, Pygmalion. And we know that King David, who ruled many years ago in Jerusalem, it will be from his lineage that the chosen one will be born, the one who will come and destroy death forever."

"He washes his garments in wine, and his clothes in the blood of grapes."

"That is what the poem teaches."

"So let's go to bed tonight believing on those sure promises of God," Hanno's mother said. Hanno's heart beat tenderly as she spoke and Pygmalion's smile of happiness caught and meshed into warmth. He felt the concreteness and deathlessness of faith past all formulations of any words that might fill the room. Pygmalion bowed his head. Hanno knew who he was praying for. He tried to pray too, but instead he began to yawn. His mother saw him and went over to prepare their sleeping mats.

Pygmalion greeted them all good night and sauntered gaily out the door, light of foot. Hanno walked to the door surveying the street and his friend's little form retreating through the embalmed darkness. Above a meteor showered by the light of the moon as from out of the shadows between the homes across the street a little dog came out and ran toward the boy.

The little dog remained in Pygmalion's custody all the way down the street, licking his hand. Hanno saw his fellow-creature disappear through the door of his home, soft, and of essence pure, and the little puppy followed him in.

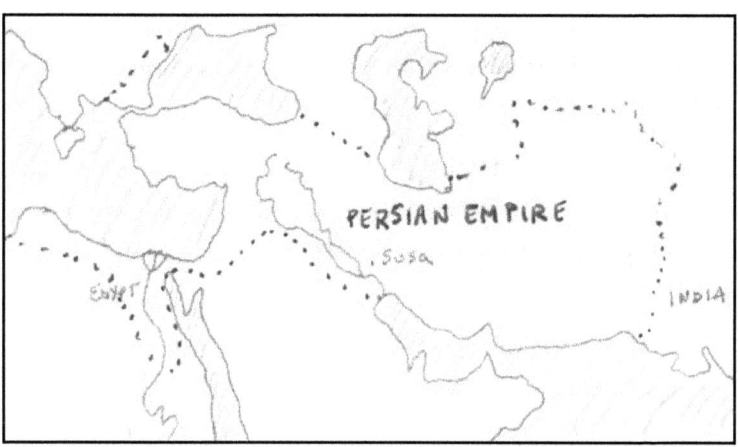

Pure Lovely

Susa, in the Persian Empire, 388 BC

1.

"Sit still, Arta!"

"But you're pulling too hard."

"I'll be careful. But you need to be more patient."

Arta's mother's nimble fingers were working Arta's hair into an intricately woven end down her back. Arta's hair was like black garlands thrown off thick in a wild curling crown. In the smooth plate used as a mirror she could see it waving in smooth coils from the front of her head. Arta could see what it would look like when it was finished by admiring her mother's braids. She had braided them first, shown them to Arta, and said, "This is how you will wear your hair to the wedding tomorrow."

"Mother?" Arta said, fingering a finely carved comb in her hands.

"Yes, dear." Her voice always seemed to be administering a kind justice, and she was ever likely to first help rather than rebuke. But there was an air of some concealed disgrace hovering beyond her. She was solemn now, and distracted, her eyes a shifting mist.

"My hair isn't as long as yours. How is it that our braids will look the same?" Arta's green eyes turned to her mother, as bright and unquenchable as the stars.

"I'll make do, darling."

Had her mother even heard the question? Arta sighed and gazed around the ornately decorated room. The big beams laced above her head uniformly in the stone-walled room. She and her mother were in the sitting room adjoining her mother and father's bedroom at the back of the house. Her eye caught the scroll on the high-up shelf beside the vanity table. All her father's scrolls were kept here. It was very dry, so they did not decay. "Maybe Father can judge," Arta told her mother.

"Yes," her mother said. "Your father can judge." Arta wasn't sure. The words that Arta's father spoke to her so seldom tended to take the shape of mountains in her young heart. But she would know what he would say soon. As soon as her father returned from the area near the old destroyed city of Nineveh, where he was on a military diplomatic mission, they would be leaving with some relatives and friends from the city to travel to the country for the wedding. Only a few more hours!

Arta's mother ran her hand down Arta's hair one final time. "Where is Kama?"

"She's playing across the street from the synagogue. Can I go?" Arta knew that her mother thought Kama had a rather untethered character, but she still let Arta play with her almost daily.

"Okay. But don't stay too late. You have to get to bed early."

Arta set the comb down next to some of her mother's gold bracelets, ready to race off. Then she stopped, and turned to her queenly mother, "Do you think the bride's hair will be like ours?"

"Yes, and more beautiful." Arta's mother laid her brush down next to the combs and sighed wearily. The bright emblazonry of her dress contrasted with her gray gaze. Her love was always there, but sometimes so contained. She seemed ready to say something, but then stopped.

"Oh, Mother," Arta said, "Don't keep worrying about the bride. God will take care of her. So what if she is marrying someone from her village?"

"Arta, surely it is a wonderful thing. And you are right, God will take care of them. They are both wishing to keep faith and a pure heart. But there are some in my family opposed to it because the bride's young man did not grow up like us. He only repented from dead works a few harvests ago."

Arta thought about this, remembering when she had heard about the young man's change of heart. His happiness had been like a brook overflowing its banks. Arta went toward the sitting-room door, ready to leave again. Then she looked up, staring at the wall above the door. On it was,

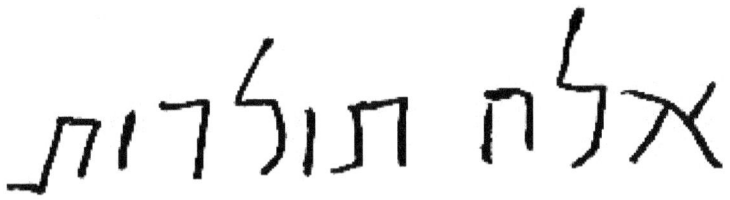

It had been there for over one hundred years. She had never asked what it meant. She knew it had something to do with time going through the generations.

"I'm only telling you this," Arta's mother was saying behind her, "so you will not argue with anyone at the wedding. No cousins, no elders, nobody. Just be quiet and patient with everyone."

Arta turned back, her hand on the door. "What should I do if someone says something rude about the bride or her young man?"

"Just tell them, there are many from India to Ethiopia who believed, since even the time of Esther. And in the psalms and in Isaiah it speaks of many people from other nations besides Judah who will believe. Now in this great kingdom of Persia that has come to pass."

"My friend Persephone is the daughter of one of the other diplomats at the palace," Arta said. "Maybe she would even come to the hearing of God's Word. She asks me ever so many questions."

"Yes, perhaps even one day the Word of God will come to the Greeks. But the Word of God is surely among many in the lands Persia rules now. The bride's young man is one of these called by grace. And all people of every country and tribe, each one of them is special and created in the image of God."

Escaped from the Nations

Arta's mother left the looking glass and walked up to Arta, giving Arta's hair one final pat. Giving her a gentle push, she said, "Now run along. You can ask your father more questions later. I have to prepare the items for the journey."

2.

Arta skipped by the big buildings of Susa. Since her father was an important official in the military buildings near the great palace of the king of Persia in Susa, she lived near the palace in one of the finest parts of the city. As she walked by a big temple of Marduk, she thought about traveling out into the country. It wasn't a far distance, it was just right outside the city, but it might as well be in Tarshish for how different it was. People in the country were mostly poor farmers. Arta's father had been a farmer, but he had been taken in by a distant cousin from the city when he was a child to learn the customs and languages of the many peoples that the Persians ruled over. He had prospered in the big city. Arta remembered her father saying once, "Even the farmers are rich in Susa."

It was true, the relatives who lived out in the country were not wealthy, but they had plenty to eat. And they were very happy. "Away from the quick and busy ways of the city," they would say. Arta's mother thought crossing over into the country was almost like crossing the River Styx, but Arta loved it. Especially at night when the sky was so bright and the fields were so open, the stars seemed to have threads running down, beckoning her to climb them.

But she loved the city too. The area she went through now was quiet and safe and wealthy, but it wasn't boring. As she went toward the synagogue, Arta walked by some others who were of her own ancestry. But there were so many others: Medes, Indians, Ethiopians, Lybians, Greeks, Phoenicians, and people from many other lands. Some were unsignalling, submissive and huddled. Others were exuberant or pedantic, or enchanting. Here a magi carried a tablet of clay. There a wise woman folded a turban. Yonder in a gated garden a young father was teaching his boy mathematics with an abacus. He reminded her of her own father, his hands motioning as if he gave a decree. As she paused in the path to watch a group of native barbarians do a ceremonial dance, Arta thought of how she didn't understand many of the adults that her father worked with. They were from this area in Persia. They were not from Judah, where Arta's family had come during the time after the Babylonians destroyed Jerusalem and carried the people away captive.

"Arta!" It was Kama. Arta had arrived at the play area down the street from her house.

Kama had golden streaks in her dark brown hair from the summer sun. It was pulled back in a jumbled bun. Her face was shiny with dust and sweat.

Arta's laugh was jolly. "Are you going to the wedding like that?"

Kama glanced down at her dirty dress. Then she lifted up her eyes to Arta, looking like a sad little sparrow.

"Kama?" Arta whispered. There was a holy conjunction between the two of them and Arta could not remember a time when she could not feel Kama's feelings keenly.

"We're not going." Kama fought back tears.

Arta gathered Kama to her in a hug. "Oh, honey."

"Mother won't say why. But I heard her and Father talking when they thought we weren't listening. They think people will talk about them badly if they go to the wedding. It is too divisive." She began to sob unreservedly, "Ah, my wedding garment! I will never wear it!"

Arta hugged her friend's narrow shoulders closer. "Oh, darling," she comforted. "There will be another wedding."

With arms entwined, the girls walked slowly toward the graveyard next to the synagogue. By habit Arta went toward the newer plots on the edge. There were the familiar graves of Stuna, Zusta, and Farnah, her brothers. Arta sat under a tuft of shade on Farnah's grave and then reached up for Kama's hand. She pulled her friend down and sat her down beside her on the graves of her brothers. All the little boys had died in infancy, but Farnah was the one Arta had held. She had never even gotten the chance to cuddle Stuna and Zusta. But Farnah had lived to be a month old. Arta remembered his sweet milky smell as she sat on the grassy grave holding Kama's hand.

Kama let go of her and motioned toward the graves. She looked around for some flowers to put on them. Finding none, she told Arta, "These little ones will never know the problems of growing up."

"Kama," Arta said, "my father says that most of those who are of our ancestry from Judah don't even believe as our forefathers, Abraham, Isaac, and Jacob, believed. Isaiah asks about this in the beginning of his writings, 'To what purpose is the multitude of your sacrifices?' They think that by following customs, and wearing certain clothes, obeying powerful people, and observing certain holidays, they will be saved. They don't talk about sin, or else they make things into sin that aren't sin. They ignore the Word and make things up to suit what satisfies their flesh. But we are saved by believing what God promises us. He promises us life with him. Look at these little boys. They are just like the little boy that King David had that died. And King David said, 'He will not come back to me, but I will go to him.'"

"I know, Arta," Kama said, waving her arms, unbraceleted and white, and bare. "My father agrees with your father. But my mother wants to have friends. So she wants to go along with the great majority of the people of Judah in this city." She reached up and touched Arta's hair. "Oh, Arta, how beautiful!"

"Yes, my mother did this."

"Your mother is so beautiful. Is she to wear all her jewelry?"

"Yes, and her best dress. We are wearing our hair the same."

"You must tell me how the bride looks when you come back."

"I will. And I'll memorize the songs."

Kama laughed, bright and unstained. "They'll be familiar songs. I am sure I will know them already."

"True. And I'll tell you how the Persian women dress and do their hair."

"Oh, Arta," Kama laughed again. "You're so funny. I see Persian women all the time."

"But, Kama, these are country women of Persia. I'm sure their ways are different. And there will be people of Egypt there too."

"Really?" Kama frowned. "Oh, I do so want to go. What do the women of Egypt wear?"

"Lots of jewelry and elaborate dresses, just like us, but different. Don't you remember the military group that our fathers let us see just a few years back? We could see from the top of the roof we were hiding on."

"Right." Kama's brow furrowed. "How are the people going to understand what the pastor is saying? Will he speak Aramaic?"

"I suppose. Father will translate into Egyptian or Ethiopian if he needs to."

"Ethiopian! Are there really Ethiopians going to be there?"

"Perhaps. There is a diplomatic group that just came in from Ethiopia and Egypt, three of them are in faith, and Father told them they're welcome to travel with us to the wedding tomorrow. There will be a sermon. They want to hear sermons."

"Will your father give them a scroll?"

"Yes, more than one, as much of the ancient stories as he can. I even heard a rumor that my cousin Mishael is to travel back to Ethiopia with them and help them, and be a pastor there."

"That's wonderful," said Kama gaily. But Arta could still hear the disappointment about the wedding in her voice.

A postman walked by the graveyard, and birds twittered and trilled above them. Arta looked at Kama's sad face and began to sing an old psalm, "Let God arise. And let his enemies be scattered."

Kama joined in. "And let them that hate him flee away before his face."

The girls' voices carried, full of heaviness and a beautiful hope, through the sevenfold quiet of the graveyard, and disappeared into the trees above as the day closed down as if surprised to be over.

3.

"It has surely come to pass," Arta's father was saying to everybody, as their group neared the small village far beyond the gates of the great city of Susa, where the wedding was to be held. Around them the countryside was lovely. The herbs and plants glistened with morning dew. Beasts of burden roamed the fields, munching on the grass. The sky seemed bigger somehow, and birds chortled everywhere in branches of the laurel and myrtle trees above.

"What, Father?" Arta asked. She had been watching a little turtle crawl across the pathway and disappear into the reeds beside the road.

"It says: And I will set a sign among them, and I will send those that escape of them unto the nations, to Tarshish, Pul, and Lud, that draw the bow, to Tubal, and Javan, to the isles afar off, that have not heard my fame, neither have seen my glory; and they shall declare my glory among the Gentiles."

"Oh. As the prophet Isaiah said so long ago."

"Yes, my child." Arta's father pointed ahead of them. "Look at all those people. There must be people from every nation going to this wedding."

"But why, Father?"

"Because there is to be preaching. People want to learn the Word of God. And there are scrolls of the books of Moses and the prophets and the Psalms to be distributed." He indicated the sky with the hand that held his travel staff. "And the weather is good. This is just the season to be able to come and listen; it is a rest, a moment to dip from the wells of salvation."

"To gather around the altar," Arta said.

"Just so, my child. We shall eat butter and honey." Arta's father gave her a little push. "Run ahead and tell the relatives we are here. I'll go help your mother with the bags."

Arta skipped ahead, waving shyly at everyone who looked her way. Some of the people here were her cousins. But she had never met many of them. They were distant cousins, and they were poor farmers. There was a kinship here, even beyond the kinship of blood. It was a fellowship of being, of using the same heart-language.

By and by, she found herself in a garden, and there was the bride under a shade, reposing on flowers, being prepared for the wedding, surrounded by her friends, her crown thick with sparkling gems and Sheba gold. She held herself still for a moment while her friends adorned her but then her animation darted and escaped. Her friends held her lovingly. Arta thought their laughter was devout, like the snow falling.

The bride's hands fluttered over the petals in her lap. Arta watched her face turning toward her attendants; the enameled color of her eyes flashed, and her lashes were beautiful. On a carpet behind her, two of the bride's sisters sewed a tear that had come into one of their own festive garments. Arta went closer to the sisters, away from the overwhelming floral scent by the bride.

"Do you think she will show up?" The younger of the bride's sisters was speaking. She was sewing a tapestry on which cherubim with two wings veiled their eyes.

"It would be a shame if she did." The older sister had light hair, a calm face, and a liquid voice of bottomless chill. She sat on an embroidered rug studded with jewels.

"No. It would be a shame if she did not." Arta's gaze was fixed on the younger sister's nodding head. It was tilted away from her, but Arta could see she had a countenance like a love poem, framed by her black hair, which was tucked into a linen covering that disguised most of it.

The younger sister must have felt Arta's gaze, because she looked up at her. Smiling, she beckoned her closer, and then addressed her sister, "I would kiss her."

"I would not." Arta heard the cold tone and wanted to think of the girl as a snaky sorceress. But she could not disagree with the harsh girl. It was her own reaction, too. She had heard her mother and father talking about Frida. And it had to be Frida that these sisters spoke of. Everyone was upset with Frida. Arta wasn't sure why, but if Frida had offended everyone, surely she was a Jezebel?

"I would ask her to sit at my table and eat with me," the younger sister was saying.

"I would not." The older sister lowered her finely-combed lashes and bent her shoulder severely away from her younger sister.

Arta saw that now the younger sister had a little baby blanket she was folding. It was soft and clean, and she was smoothing it tenderly.

"Darling, what is it?" It was the voice of the bride, coming like a signal. She had noticed Arta staring and eavesdropping.

Arta blushed at being addressed. "Nothing," she said, turning away.

"Darling?"

Arta fled. The younger sister's cheery voice dulled to nothing behind her as she darted down the walkway toward where the newly arrived guests were gathering. Scrolls were being laid out on wooden tables on the grass. Arta saw one title. It said, "The Book of Gad the Seer." A man led a group of foreigners through them, explaining them. As Arta went toward them, just beyond the scrolls, in the kitchen area, she saw her mother.

"Mother?" Moving past the scrolls, Arta stopped in front of her mother, who was stirring a large pot that smelled of meat. Her face shone from the steam coming up out of the pot.

"Arta, there you are. Go and hold that baby. He's right over there."

Arta took a rowdy baby boy out of the arms of a red-haired Persian farmer girl. The girl was so young she staggered under the weight of the fat baby. Arta smiled at her, and waved her away. The girl scampered off. Tucking the little boy's clothes around him, and brushing off his dusty feet, Arta put him on her hip and went back to her mother.

"Mother. Why do some people not like Frida?"

Arta's mother looked around the room. She put her finger to her lips. Arta saw her two aunts had gone quiet across the kitchen. Questions brimmed in their eyes. Her pulse sank.

The little boy in her arms began wailing.

"Come here, Arta, come stir this."

Arta stirred while her mother calmed the little boy. As he stilled, Arta's mother looked at her two aunts across the room. They were chatting quietly again. Arta's mother bent her head and said, "Arta, you must learn to speak quietly."

"But, mother, what is wrong with Frida?"

"Nothing. But she has no father for this little boy."

"What? This little baby is Frida's?"

"We are trying to find out what happened. She disappeared at harvest time and came back after two winters. Who knows what happened. She wouldn't say. We would like to help someone marry Frida. The little boy needs a father."

Arta's mother's eyes shimmered with sadness, and she looked unseeing at Arta. Then she said in a settled tone, "Darling, do not consider it so deeply, don't look so fatal-visaged. And please don't ask me any more questions about the matter. Just be kind to Frida if you see her. And be kind to everyone."

"Is she my cousin, Mother?"

"Frida? Not a close cousin, but yes, I suppose she is a cousin, in a way, through marriage."

"Oh. Mother?"

"Yes?"

"I saw ever so many tablets with writing on them stacked in a caravan next to ours as we arrived. Do you think there are any stories on them?"

"Stories? I suppose so, but you'll have to wait until the evening storytelling. You must not touch those tablets."

"Yes, Mother." Arta took the little boy out of her mother's arms. He was quiet as a figure on a marble urn, but his face was covered with dirt and dried tears. "Let's go find your mother," she told him.

4.

Arta's arms ached from carrying the chubby baby around while looking all over for his mother. Seeing a crowd gathered around a tree, she went toward it. There a man was saying, "But Ezekiel said it straight out, 'But the house of Israel will not hearken unto thee.' So Ezekiel got told by God that he had to go preach to people who God knew were not going to hear him."

Arta got closer and saw that the man speaking those words was a huge Ethiopian. He was not old, but he had fearsome eyes and flashing gold jewels at his throat and ears. Gathered around him, under the big oak with shading limbs and fading leaves, were seven or so others.

A skinny boy, barely out of childhood and severe in his youthful beauty, waved his arms as if he could convince the big Ethiopian just by his humming intensity. His gestures transfixed Arta. "So they were so hard-hearted and he knew this," the boy said. "He knew what was going on in their hearts."

"No. He didn't." The big Ethiopian was still sitting but he looked like he was going to get up, a giant obelisk, smooth as a swan. Arta could see him curling his fingers into his hands, a sharp ring on one finger almost cutting his palm.

"God told him." The skinny boy was adamant, the wind fanning his curls coolly as his voice rose, disintegrated and tempestuous above rule or art. "So he knew." Arta found herself leaning back from his ferventness.

The Ethiopian's reply was patient, mild as a sparrow, or a blue summer sky. "Even if God tells you something about someone, you can still hope when there is no hope, and go forward in hope. It says in Joshua that Joshua told the people, 'Ye cannot serve the Lord, for he is a holy God. He is a jealous God. He will not forgive you your transgressions, nor your sins.' And what did the people say, even hearing this? They said, 'But we will serve the Lord.' For it says in Joel 'And rend your heart, and not your garments, and turn unto the LORD your God: for he is gracious and merciful, slow to anger, and of great kindness, and repenteth him of the evil. Who knoweth if he will return and repent, and leave a blessing behind him; even a meat offering and a drink offering unto the LORD your God?' We should live in hope."

The skinny boy, who, by his accent, Arta could tell was from India, finally got up. He moved closer to the Ethiopian, undisturbed that he was a third of the man's size. "But sir . . . ," he began.

"Gentlemen, please." The voice was like a stone loosening and beginning to roll down a hill. It came from behind Arta. Her head whipped around. "Father!" she whispered.

"The whole head is sick and the whole heart is faint," Arta's father muttered. The others had stopped at his voice.

Arta shut her eyes, wondering. Then she opened them, considering the Ethiopian and the boy from India again. The Ethiopian's majestic smile was in his eyes, and reached out to the young man from India, whose other waving hand fell to his side. His curly hair was stuck to his forehead and he stared with a frantic intentness outward. He turned as if to leave the circle but then he stopped himself, and threw his arms around the big Ethiopian.

"Little children," he said, "let us love one another." Then calmly he scanned the faces of the audience, then the Ethiopian's. "Now, what other passages of Scripture do you have to support your claims?"

Arta's father backed away from the two of them. He sat down in the grass next to Arta and settled in to listen beneath the sky that was like a moat surrounding them all and keeping them in.

"Well," Arta's father motioned to the Ethiopian and the boy from India, "go on."

The two disputers did not say anything for a moment. The vestiges of battle dulled to lassitude as the heat from the copper sun intensified. The big Ethiopian rose like a bubble coming to the surface and moved further into the shade. The boy from India only gazed at him, uncomprehending, deep in thought like a sphinx. All sat musing and discussing the matter in low tones. Then a voice came from those who had gathered to watch the discussion.

"The Ethiopian is right." It was a young girl as beautiful as the bride. Arta realized she had been sitting there all along.

"Father," she whispered, "that's Frida, isn't it?"

"Yes, child."

Arta watched as Frida talked. Her tone was like poured cream. She quoted the writings of Moses. The Ethiopian was completely silent. He looked like he had been caught out in something bright. He sat near Arta and she could see he wore an ornate gold signet ring. The boy from India, further away from where Arta was, was answering Frida, but he answered without waving his hands. Just his voice came, softly.

Arta moved closer to Frida, because more people had gathered around to listen. But Frida fell silent and the big Ethiopian and the boy from India began again. Some of the people listening were translating what was being said to others, so there was a constant quiet fluttering of sound all around even though they were all trying to disturb the debate as little as possible.

"The Ethiopian is right," Arta's father said to everyone after listening for a few more minutes. "There are many things we don't know. We do not harvest the corners of the field. We leave them into charity. We have to function as if everyone is about to receive the grace of repentance and enter into mercy as we have."

"But what if God says, and tells us, that another person hates him, hates God, and will betray him?" It was the boy from India.

"God says those kinds of things to let us know that it is possible that a heart can become so dull and numb and blaspheming that it is past hope. But why does Joel say, 'Who knoweth?' He means this, we are never to decide—we don't know and we never know until God decides. And it is us, surely, who are the betrayers." As he spoke, his hands lifted, then dropped, velvety, like an ephemeral question.

The young man from India sat back. People began to speak in small groups. Arta turned to her father, "Father, it's just like a debate in the synagogue, isn't it?"

Arta's father sighed. "No, Arta," he said, "no, it's not."

"Father, why?"

Arta's father looked around. The little red-haired girl had come up to the group. Seeing Arta she looked relieved and went up to her, taking the little boy from Arta's arms. Arta glanced at Frida, who was now speaking quickly and firmly in Greek to another young woman who had been listening to the entire discussion.

"This is Frida's baby, isn't it, Father?"

"Yes, darling." Arta's father touched the forehead of the placid little boy and nodded at the little red-haired girl. "And that's why it's not like a synagogue discussion. Frida would never be there if it was. Neither would you. And," he said suddenly, as if he had taken into his hand a live coal, "neither would I."

Arta's father was speaking Hebrew, and Arta noticed nobody could understand him except her. Arta looked around at the crowd. "I suppose the Ethiopian wouldn't be there either. Or the boy from India. Or that Greek."

"Moabites, Edomites, children of bastards—they are not to enter into the assembly. The men at synagogue don't understand Moses. They take this instruction from Moses about foreigners and twist it. Moses meant spiritual Moabites, spiritual Edomites, spiritual adulterers. But they don't understand. They wash their hands, but not their hearts. Their hearts have returned to Egypt."

5.

The early evening was yellow and rose. The final notes of the final song of the wedding hovered for a final second and then fled. The groom took the bride's hand and led her to the carpet in the front of the room in a frothing rush of linen, embroidery, gems, and gold. The two sat with their heads bent together as the sermon began beneath the open sky by a stream. The lute-player near Arta caressed her instrument gently as the sun around them bathed the soil in warmth.

The colors and the music, and the upraised countenances of the wedding guests were too compelling for Arta. The sound of the sermon seemed far away. Arta closed her eyes over the scene for a moment, trying to picture it so she could describe it in detail to Kama when she got back home.

She counted and saw that more than half of the people at the wedding were her relatives, people whose ancestors had come from Judah long ago. But the Ethiopian and his wife fascinated Arta, as did the boy from India. He sat next to the Ethiopian, Arta noticed, and one of the little children of the Ethiopian had fallen asleep in his lap.

Both the Ethiopian and the boy from India were riveted to the preacher's words. Arta studied the preacher for a moment. He was her relative, an old man; his Aramaic had a Hebrew tone to it. Behind the Ethiopian and the boy from India a big group of Persians sat, some of them leaning toward a man who was interpreting the sermon for them. They seemed to be chewing on the words that were being spoken, Arta thought.

Arta looked behind her. In the very back on the edge of the crowd she saw Frida. Her little boy was sleeping in her arms.

"And so," the minister was saying, "he shall arise and shake terribly the earth. But the Lord of hosts will be a little sanctuary for us."

Arta scrutinized him. Was it over already? What had the preacher said?

"Let us pray."

Arta bowed her head, sneaking a look out of the corner of her eye at Frida. The whole assembly of wedding guests felt joined together in watchfulness. Frida's head was bowed, too.

"Rejoice ye with Jerusalem, and be glad with her, all ye that love her. Rejoice for joy with her, all ye that mourn for her."

Arta noticed that Frida's little boy had woken up. Next to her the bride's older sister, as a tangled tragedy, glared at him. The older sister would no sooner leap clear of a jealous thought that it would jump her again. Behind her passionless glare was a crouching, a cowering. But Frida did not see it. She was smiling and her countenance trembled with a beautiful convulsion of longing for the rest that the preacher had spoken of. Frida rocked her little boy, and the older sister slunk away from the wedding with a final gaze as the talons of a harpy, as if it was a festival in a war she had never known.

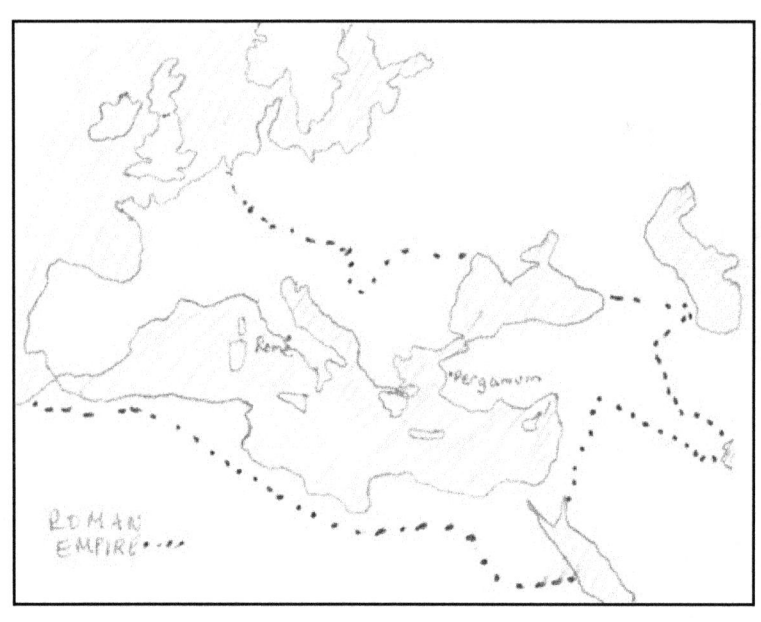

Blessed Are the Meek

Pergamum, in the Roman Empire, AD 44

1.

THE COLD SLIPPED AWAY unwillingly from the earth, and the fogs passing away made manifest an army on the hills, resting. The tiles on the picture of the scene were cool as Claudius ran his hands across them, almost feeling the sharp cold of the sword in the soldier's hand who was nearest him in the foreground of the large mosaic. He stood back a moment and scanned up across the entire panorama of the military scene made timeless in the wall of the atrium. He couldn't reach the prancing horses on the hills behind the army. They were too high up. But he imagined their distress during the battle.

"Where is that lazy scamp?" The voice like a satyr's came from behind the row of pillars outside in the garden.

Claudius stumbled toward his wash-bucket, fleeing, as when Ulysses shunned Charybdis. He got on his knees and put his hands into the soapy lukewarm water. As he squeezed the rag, the master of slaves came in.

"You're not done in here yet?" The master of slaves came near and rested his hand on Claudius's head, flattening his curls. Claudius could hear his slow inhaling, and smell his cloying perfume. Claudius held himself very still, as if threatened in the wide womb of an uncreated night. The hand of the master of slaves on his head did not move in the acrid air. It was as if immobilizing Claudius's head in a frieze as still as the mosaic across the atrium. Claudius fixed his gaze on the pavement of marble and the roof of dim crossbeams.

Claudius remembered his colorful and furious dream from the night before, of a fire that clung to the walls of his room and licked at his feet. The hand of the master of slaves moved, almost caressingly through Claudius's curls, to settle on his forehead. Claudius knew himself to be in the presence of a brutal and unbarred wickedness. He lifted his hands out of the bucket carefully and smoothed the washrag over its edge with the deliberate movements of aching steps over burnt mud.

"Does the master require me, sir? Or the pedagogue?" His whispered voice was like a surprise witness against the visage and stature of the master of slaves.

Claudius felt the hand slide over his curls one more time and out of his hair. He got up and backed away from the master of slaves, ignoring the panting.

"Yes," said the master of slaves. "The pedagogue requires you for help with the geometry lesson."

Claudius felt the eyes of the master of slaves finally fall off his back as he disappeared behind a cracked pillar in the garden. He went across the courtyard, through sunny rows of flowers and into the other side of the home, then upstairs and down a hall toward the schoolroom.

There was only one child of the home, Jason. He was two years older than Claudius. Claudius did as he always did as he approached Jason. He slowed down and listened. The schoolroom door was open but as Claudius stood just outside it and out of view, he could hear no sound but a low scratching. He waited until it stopped, moving closer to the door. Finally, he looked in. There was the turbulent and sensual Jason, slumped over with his head on the table in front of him in a drunken sleep. It was a beautiful table, and had previously been used to lay out the bodies of those downed in combat.

Across the room at another writing desk facing them, the teacher's head moved, bent over, first to read the book on his left, then to copy out a comment on it carefully onto the empty paper to his right. On the wall above him was etched a saying, "Homo homini lupus," it said. "Man is a wolf to man."

Claudius walked past the empty seat where the pedagogue sometimes sat. He took the chair next to Jason's.

The scratching of the teacher's pen came, with mechanical relentlessness. Then came the pause, then more scratching—the only sound in the room. The spring wind kept the smells of the city at bay outside. The public holiday today meant everyone was out celebrating in the streets. The pedagogue had probably let Jason get drunk even though it was early afternoon, so he could go out to the celebrations. Jason's father was in Corinth for business and his mother was visiting her sister in a village outside of Philippi. She had been visiting for three years, ever since Jason had lit fire to her bedroom.

Claudius turned toward the snoring Jason. He smelled of vomit. Under his arm Claudius saw the corner of some worn pages. The teacher at the front of the room continued reading and scratching his pen across the parchment as tireless as a spider. Claudius tugged on the pages under Jason's arm. Jason shifted in his sleep and Claudius got the pages out from under his arm. He looked at what was on the page and could not look away. It was like an invisible grip, like the master of slaves holding his head toward the pictures on the page.

His heart beat and the pounding finally pierced through to his brain. He flipped the pages over onto the grape-stained desk, closing his eyes and breathing in deeply.

He stared at the back page, the images burning into his mind. Getting up and grabbing a blank stack of paper from the shelf nearby he took it and placed it over Jason's evil pictures. He gazed toward the window, then toward the teacher, whose pen was still scratching. Claudius watched him turn the parchment over and begin reading again, the top of his bald head sunburned from the unexpected spring sunshine on yesterday's exercise excursion.

Claudius didn't have to go over and check what sort of writing the man was doing. It was something about how no measure was of any use unless attended by fear and the expectation of punishment, surely.

Claudius turned back to the shelf and pulled out the geometry problems they had been looking at yesterday. The letters and numbers and diagrams swam all over the page in front of him. He watched as the corner of the carefully drawn graph from yesterday blurred into a pool of oblivion and slid apart. His salty tear moved it in a river across the page and onto the old carved table.

2.

"Claudius!" The word dripped with the entrails of dissatisfaction.

"Yes, Jason." Claudius answered with shy dignity, as always.

"Hail horrors. Where is everyone?" Jason rubbed his eyes and scanned the room for a wine bottle. Seeing one across the room he went and drank from it. It was still about one-third full. Claudius looked down at his geometry, waiting for Jason to get drunk. The teacher at the front of the room kept reading and copying. Jason drank more, as if by drinking he could tie himself to the mast. His fine blondish hair straggled down uncut into his handsome but bloated features. He looked like his father, massive, though only still a teenager, massy, large, and muscular, the associate and co-partner of his father's loss.

His fleshy lips pursed, and he licked their generousness as he watched the people dancing in the street below. The cavorting crowd below him was like something from the theatre.

"They prefer what is only a life for cattle," he sneered.

The loud cries of someone getting hurt below brought a hiss of laughter. But Claudius knew that Jason was no longer even capable of loving Jason's own terror, if he had any. Claudius had never seen a brutal smile last long on Jason's face, even as he watched gladiators tear each other apart in the arena. Claudius often watched Jason, instead of the action in the coliseum. When he had been younger he had been able to tell the degree of gore in the theatre scene based on Jason's facial expressions. But no more. Now they were always set the same.

"What's it all for, Claudius? What is the final end? To contemplate the absolute Idea alone?" Jason had once asked him. A whore had died one night, killed by one of Jason's best friends. Claudius remembered the red right hand of Jason's companion. Nothing came of it, it was a slave whore. It had been almost in another country, and besides, the wench was dead. "Why did she run off and then have the baby? Why not expose it like a decent woman should?"

"Well, what does Aristotle say?" asked Claudius in reply.

"That youth are inclined to restlessness and stupidity of thought."

"Yes."

"And from the *Antigone* and in *Oedipus Rex* it is clear we are to understand that fate is unescapable fate. But what happens when I die?"

"Die?" Claudius thought of the dead babies in the trash heaps of the city. Flies were born from their decaying bodies, he knew. He asked Jason, "Well, you mean the dead babies in the garbage?"

"No, not them."

"What then?"

"It is true that those are the only dead humans I have seen. I mean, I have read about the death of Socrates, and how he says there is life after death, and we are judged then, by what we have done in this life, whether it is good or bad. But to go to be with the gods, to drink ambrosia—what do you think, Ganymede, is that all true? Some people say it isn't."

Claudius shut his eyes. Where had those dead babies gone? Their bodies rotted and stank among the trash. "You mean does their soul go to be with the gods even though their bodies have died?"

"Yes."

"I don't know. I suspect that if anyone goes to be with the gods it would be those little babies."

"Oh, do get off the babies—they're nothings. Slave rot."

"They're human beings like you and me."
"They're the offspring of brutes."
"Well, so am I."
"You don't know who your father and mother are. You're an orphan we found. But you weren't a little baby. You were four. And smart. You make a good slave." By that time Jason had drained a cup and a half of wine.

Claudius got up and took the container from him. He set it near the bust of Livy and then led Jason to a reclining couch in the corner of the school room and sat him down. He bent down and unstrapped Jason's sandals. "This is the active exercise of my soul's facilities, eh, Claudius?" Jason muttered.

Setting the sandals in the corner, Claudius returned to Jason's reclining couch. He kneeled down and smoothed Jason's tangled hair out of his long eyelashes. "Jason," he had said. "Sleep now, my friend. God will help us."

"God." Jason's eyes had flickered for a moment. "Which one?"

"The unknown God." Then Claudius took one last look at the teacher, who was still copying at the table in the front of the room. Then he sneaked into the dark hallway and up to the corner closet on the top floor in his ragged linen garment.

3.

When he came back an hour later, Jason stood at the window again looking at the street scene below. The teacher's "scratch, scratch" went on at the table in the front of the room. Jason tried to walk toward Claudius but staggered and tripped on a chair, almost falling. The teacher made no sign that he even recognized Jason and Claudius were in the room.

"Claudius," Jason said, "let's go down to the party."

"Please, no, Jason. You can hardly walk. It's getting dark. It gets worse and worse as it gets dark. Don't make me go with you."

"Afraid?" Jason's attention was uncanny and drugged.

"Yes."

"I'll kill anyone who grabs you."

"Please, Master Jason. I don't want to go. And it's not safe for you, either."

Jason laughed, with witching restlessness. "The worst things have already happened to me. And I can easily put a knife in anybody."

"Don't speak of it, Master Jason. We can stay here. Come, I'll read you some Herodotus."

"The wars of Cyrus again?" Jason dug around in the corner and found another cup of wine. He tipped a little of it into his mouth. Some spilled out and made a crimson stain across the front of his purple toga.

"Your father will let you go to the forum and hear the cases argued with him if you finish Herodotus, Jason."

"My father. Who is my father? He doesn't even care enough to buy me a decent pedagogue. The man doesn't watch me. He never did. He never will."

"Would you rather he hit you? Many boys have pedagogues who beat them."

Jason's face was dark and purplish. "Yes."

"Your father loves you. You will inherit all things from him. He only wishes you to do your lessons."

"He hates me." Jason stepped madly into the table, slamming the wine cup down on it.

Claudius had never feared that Jason would hit him, but suddenly he feared the wildness of reaping the whirlwind.

He got up and slunk toward the open door. "Jason," he pleaded, "do let's get you to bed. You will pass out."

Jason followed Claudius into the doorway, leaning against the pillar.

Some cure or charm had suddenly taken hold of him, soothing. A look crossed his face that Claudius had never seen. He was almost calm. In that moment Claudius loved him more than he had ever loved him before. Jason, who had killed the assistant of the master of slaves because Claudius had been so afraid of him. He had never told Jason why and the horror had never grown mild. But Jason had known, and had murdered the man, wearing his blood to the dinner table.

Jason slid down against the pillar and hid his face in his hands.

"Tomorrow you will go with me?"

Claudius was crying. He couldn't understand why, but he took Jason's big shoulder and touched his chin. Jason's head lolled and he was biting his lip. Claudius wiped the blood away and then put his little arms around Jason's body, soaked with wine, sweat, and vomit.

"Where, Jason?"

"Tomorrow, you'll go with me."

"All right, Jason. I'll go with you." Claudius tried to lift him. "Come, my friend," he pleaded. "Come."

Jason struggled to his feet and Claudius led him down the stairs and through the darkening olive garden over to his room. Jason slumped onto the bed. Claudius covered him with a light blanket.

"Jason, where?" he shook him.

Jason just drooled.

Claudius climbed up the stairs to his bed. Outside the sky began to wet the earth with soft falling showers. He lit a flame and tried to read some more Herodotus. He turned away from the pages for a moment, leaving the fire lit. All he could see were the images on the table, partially covered by Jason's arm. He felt the pictures come groping at him, and suddenly he was more afraid than when the master of slaves had held his head for those moments in the atrium. He shut his eyes again, but the pictures from the parchment turned into pictures of dead babies on trash heaps. The babies' faces were pale and unmoving, like beatitudes past utterance, but their little hands reached out to Claudius. Then, just as their little cold fingers were curling around his warm hand, they were pulled away as the harpies screeched and the hands of Jason gleamed red in the moonlight as he stood over the dead body of a slave. Claudius shuddered. He scratched the scab on his shoulder where the master of slave's assistant had gouged him last week with his long womanly fingernails.

"Claudius."

It was Jason, standing in the doorway, his eyes reflecting the moon. He had that same intense demonic and ecstatic waiting look, like an actor on the theatre's stage who was no longer acting. Outside a storm with all its battering engines beat as if to raze the area.

"Claudius."

"Yes, Jason."

"Tomorrow we are going to the synagogue." Then Jason passed away into the darkness and Claudius thought of how the sleeping and the dead are both as pictures. He went to his bed and laid down. The room was dark and there was no lamp lit. The moon was the only light. But if there had been a lamp, it would have lit up the face of the boy that was like the face of an inexplicable angel.

The sleepy drench of the forgetful lake closed in when Claudius shut his eyes. The sordid images of which his soul seemed to be constituted were blessedly gone for a moment. Even in the dark, Claudius's face arrested; it was a face that had so seized Jason's father when he saw him standing by the alleyway in the slave-market, that he had been compelled to pay double the price for him.

Biblical References

The Visitation

Genesis 1:1—11:23

Shining in Our Hearts

Exodus 14:31—40:38
Numbers 9:15—16:2
Psalm 105:17-22

My Beautiful Home

2 Samuel 2:1—2 Samuel 21:22
Ezekiel 16:3

Crying after Him

1 Kings 5:6
1 Kings 16:28—2 Kings 9:37
1 Chronicles 22:4
2 Chronicles 2:14
2 Chronicles 21:12-15
Ezekiel 27:8
Obadiah 1:20
Luke 4:26

BIBLICAL REFERENCES

Pure Lovely

Esther 8:16–17
Isaiah 45:14

Blessed Are the Meek

Acts 1:8

www.ingramcontent.com/pod-product-compliance
Lightning Source LLC
Chambersburg PA
CBHW070934160426
43193CB00011B/1686